T0267167

For all leaders who are too busy to grieve, dreamers who can't find rest, and outcasts who have run the race of rejection but can't seem to hurdle acceptance: this carefully written work is like a pedicure designed for "beautiful feet" according to the Bible.

Mitchell West (Street Hymns), author, battle rapper, disciple-maker, and spoken word artist

Face Forward is an extraordinary guide for anyone feeling stuck or weighed down by the burdens of life. With unparalleled grit and tenacity, Bethny delivers a profound and transformative message that resonates deeply with those seeking a path forward. Rather than focusing on her personal losses, she courageously shifts the narrative to highlight the invaluable lessons learned along the way. This book is a testament to resilience and the human spirit, offering readers not just hope but also a powerful blueprint for overcoming life's challenges and having the courage to see God through it all. The wisdom in these pages was hard-fought for, and the strength that Bethny lends to readers was produced through deep wrestling. Bethny is a voice that both cuts through the marrow and bone of our spirit with conviction but also mends them back together with gracious empathy.

Charaia Rush, author of *Courageously Soft*

Face Forward is a masterfully written testament to the shared human experience, humbly offering practical wisdom for readers to face life's trials and everyday moments with God's grace, free from judgment and fear. Bethny Ricks's vulnerability taps into our deepest challenges without seeking pity, but instead weaving a powerful narrative of strength and faith. Bethny authentically makes each reader feel part of the journey, ensuring that everyone will see themselves in this book and emerge as a better version of themselves.

Luke A. Fedlam, sports attorney

I have the privilege of knowing Bethny outside of her successful career, and *Face Forward* reads not like the coaching of a renowned leadership expert (she is) but like a tender heart-to-heart from a friend that I know and hold dear. She has invited us into both her fine-tuned expertise and her deeply loving heart. She has given us the keys not just to success on this side of heaven but also to the fulfillment that can only come from the other. She has cracked her life wide open and laid bare the wisdom of her experiences and the hard-fought hopefulness that comes from knowing her Father in heaven. For those of us caught looking behind, Bethny invites us to the hopeful journey forward and shows us the victory that is possible and, by God's grace, eminent, even after we stumble.

Jasmine Holmes, author of *Yonder Come Day*, *Crowned with Glory*, and others

Bethny Ricks's book delves beyond inspiration, immersing you in a profound journey of vulnerability and guidance, leading to a transformative awakening and a deep rediscovery of purpose. Like a trusted guide, she walks alongside you on this soul-stirring exploration that unravels layers of self-discovery and ignites a lasting metamorphosis within you.

Mariela Rosario, author; founder of She Speaks Fire

FACE
FORWARD

FACE FORWARD

RECLAIMING HOPE
WHEN **EVERYTHING** FALLS APART

BETHNY RICKS

ZONDERVAN REFLECTIVE

Face Forward
Copyright © 2024 by Bethny Ricks

Published in Grand Rapids, Michigan, by Zondervan. Zondervan is a registered trademark of The Zondervan Corporation, L.L.C., a wholly owned subsidiary of HarperCollins Christian Publishing, Inc.

Requests for information should be addressed to customercare@harpercollins.com.

Zondervan titles may be purchased in bulk for educational, business, fundraising, or sales promotional use. For information, please email SpecialMarkets@Zondervan.com.

ISBN 978-0-310-15724-3 (audio)

Library of Congress Cataloging-in-Publication Data

Names: Ricks, Bethny, author.
Title: Face forward : reclaiming hope when everything falls apart / Bethny Ricks.
Description: Grand Rapids, Michigan : Zondervan, 2024.
Identifiers: LCCN 2024007659 (print) | LCCN 2024007660 (ebook) | ISBN 9780310157229 (hardcover) | ISBN 9780310157236 (ebook)
Subjects: LCSH: Faith. | Hope—Religious aspects—Christianity. | Self-actualization (Psychology)—Religious aspects—Christianity. | Leadership—Religious aspects—Christianity. | Christian life.
Classification: LCC BV4637 .R48 2024 (print) | LCC BV4637 (ebook) | DDC 234/.23—dc23/eng/20240404
LC record available at https://lccn.loc.gov/2024007659
LC ebook record available at https://lccn.loc.gov/2024007660

Any internet addresses (websites, blogs, etc.) and telephone numbers in this book are offered as a resource. They are not intended in any way to be or imply an endorsement by Zondervan, nor does Zondervan vouch for the content of these sites and numbers for the life of this book.

Names and identifying characteristics of some individuals have been changed to preserve their privacy.

Published in association with The Bindery Agency, www.TheBinderyAgency.com.

Cover design: Thinkpen Design
Cover photo: Agape Media
Interior design: Sara Colley

Printed in the United States of America

24 25 26 27 28 LBC 5 4 3 2 1

Dedicated with love and gratitude to the real MVPs—my parents, Robin and Shelia. Your unwavering support is the secret sauce. To my fantastic siblings, Norlin, Collin, Dayna, and Jamie—thanks for the endless laughs and the ongoing debate over who holds the title of the favorite child (spoiler alert: it's definitely me).

*Denise, your influence
remains immeasurable.*

*This book reflects the profound impact
you've had on my life and others.*

CONTENTS

A BEGINNING

DEEP BREATHS

It was rainy, and I was scared. My neck felt so stiff I worried it might break under the weight of my thoughts. My back teeth carried the brunt of the tension building inside my head. This would certainly trigger another migraine. I was overwhelmed by the whirlwind of my life. Something needed to give as I walked the razor-thin edge of acknowledging just how alone I felt.

The only logical thing I could think to do was to walk into the rain and stand there until I was soaked. So that's precisely what I did. I imagined that underneath this curtain I would feel closer to God. I might find some semblance of strength. *Then* I could face the relentless needling of the mounting pressures barreling my way, the failures staring back.

Maybe in the rain all the uncertainty would wash away.

"At least I have enough presence of mind to put on rain boots first," I thought. A small gesture of control in the chaos. The hard rubber from the boots hit my bare knees, reminding me of the chill awaiting outside and that I certainly was not dreaming. I needed mercy. I needed something to overpower all my senses and remind me of God's tender embrace. I needed to find some hint of hope in the rain.

The drops felt warm and heavy as they pounded my weary shoulders. Hard enough, they seemed to bounce before crashing onto the black pavement. My breathing was labored. I was confused, angry, and exhausted. I had too many feelings to manage, with no remaining dark and empty corners in which to tuck away my troubles.

The Bible tells us not to worry about tomorrow, for it will worry about itself. Each day has enough trouble of its own (Matthew 6:34). But as I stood fighting to preserve parts of myself, yesterday, today, and tomorrow were collapsing. God seemed so distant. "What happens in this situation, God?" I asked. "Where do I cast all these cares?" And then I remembered: *My husband will be home soon.*

A familiar fear surfaced.

My marriage had grown volatile. Lately, its toxicity had begun spinning out of control. I could no longer keep a lid on what was happening behind the doors of my beautiful home. Divorce was imminent.

My hip bones locked into place from the cold. I mumbled incoherent thoughts because I had no shoulder to lean on. I didn't care if my neighbors saw. I had earned this flash of panic, the right to crack under the weight of parenting, leading, repeatedly crawling out of the trenches, and jumping the mental hurdles of accomplishment. All I had was this single, brief moment. So I stood. Mumbling in the rain. To a God who did not seem in a rush to respond.

Have you ever had a time when you knew everything in your life was about to change but you were unsure if it would be for the better? Have you questioned the doors God has opened because of how you fumbled previous choices? Have you ever stood on a thin line between the old and new chapters of your life, wondering how it would all unfold? Shuffling through everything you thought you knew as you suddenly became unfamiliar with your own story?

Trembling and holding unanswered questions, I turned my eyes toward heaven and dared to open

them. The rain blended nicely with the tears stream-
ing down my face—both danced away from the
pain in my dark brown eyes and the faint lines on
my face.

These lines had been etched from silent stress,
life in the trenches, and sleepless nights. They say the
physical body keeps the score, but it was my mind on
the ropes. I wondered how long my body and mind
could carry the load.

"Where are you, God? My crazy is showing," I
thought.

Tomorrow the news would be out: I was being
promoted to the position of senior vice president.
This news should have been positive, but I knew
better. The climb to this position had been too challenging. My peers had become enemies, and friends
grew distant. Somewhere along the way, the goal had
become about proving everyone wrong, including my
uneasiness. Anxiety had taken root years prior in
my career, nurtured by both leaders and so-called
professional coaches. At the peak of my journey,
I found myself burdened by relentless questions:
"What if I fail?" and "What if I can't bounce back
after failing?" The acknowledgment of a fractured
marriage only added to this drumbeat. Soon I would
truly be doing this all alone.

Despite my professional achievements, growing financial bandwidth, and the accolades for my dedication, words from the past haunted me. Being the only Black woman in corporate spaces is difficult. Being the youngest executive adds an additional layer of complexity. Deciding to operate with conviction and integrity can create even more pressure. Throughout my career, I was periodically told, "If you fail, you will ruin it for those behind you"—a sucker punch that landed each time I heard it.

I knew it wasn't wholly true. No single person is the precedent setter for younger women, people of color, Black executives, or women looking to advance above a corporate manager level. Yet here I was, trembling in the rain. Wrestling with deposits made by the ill-intended, prejudiced, and misled. Fighting to deny the self-doubt I had carried into this moment of vulnerability. Trying to find my voice and faded boundary lines.

During the climb to the top, in and out of the peaks and valleys I had become lost in the fog. I often lost sight of my passions and personal goals, assuming there was some reprieve to be found at these new finish lines. Buried somewhere within the opinions of people and professional accomplishments I hoped to find peace, acceptance, and a freedom that cannot always be defined with words. But now I knew no rest would be found at this peak. All I saw were bigger mountains with no place to hide and endless valleys with no shortcuts.

"I am so tired. God could fix this so quickly," I thought with anger.

As I came back to myself, a sharp pain wrapped around my side. I was cold, and the curls in my hair were frozen from the chill in the breeze. "Why am I doing this alone, God? Have you left me again? Where are you?" I was struggling not only to gain clarity but also to move forward. As the soft wind carried my words away, I bit my chapped bottom lip, pulling at the wayward skin with my front teeth.

"I need to shower," I thought.

I had to get dinner started and prepare a short speech because in twelve hours I would be walking through a door God had obviously kicked off its hinges. As I walked toward the entryway of the house, my mind remained in shambles. *Pull it together, Bethny.*

Now I was wet, and my situation appeared no different. I'd had no epiphanies, gotten no immediate comfort, and discovered no solid answers. I was still drowning under the growing list of fears, doubts, and shame attempting to take me under.

As I locked the front door and removed my boots, the garage door lifted, jolting me, once again, back into familiar rhythms.

SEE YOUR WAY CLEAR

Navigating the tumultuous paths of life, laden with pain, scraped knees, and clenched teeth, is indeed challenging. Yet within this difficulty, there exists a profound assurance: God's love transcends every bruise, mistreatment, and setback. It holds a power that eclipses our failures, dispels the shadows of distorted views, and cuts through the constant distractions that seek to divert our focus.

In our journey to prepare for life's unexpected moments, we seek wisdom from various resources, absorbing knowledge from books, articles, podcasts, and the wisdom of mentors. Yet, despite our efforts, we often find ourselves searching for courage amid life's dirt roads and deep trenches, standing at the precipice of choice, wondering how we strayed so far from our center—the place where God provides unwavering strength and rest.

This book acknowledges our struggles and aims to empower you to release the grip of dependency, abandon false hopes, and navigate away from the allure of indecision that leaves you in a fog of doubt. By understanding that maintaining faith, confronting failure head-on, and overcoming obstacles are messy—not because God is absent but because life is intricate, layered, and complex—you will feel yourself transitioning to empowered decision-making with each page turn, ready to confront challenges with renewed clarity and courage.

In each chapter, we dive deep into experiences, peeling back layers to better examine our footsteps with an honesty often absent in mainstream narratives. It asks the essential question: What if someone passionately encouraged you to embrace failure, uncover the majesty of God amid chaos, and take control of your life by sharing their own glaring imperfections without self-deprecation? And through this type of exploration, you will glean insights that lead to greater confidence and resiliency to overcome life's unforeseen twists and turns.

As a woman of God, unbroken by life's trials, I've waded through trenches seeking help, experiencing silence, yet never blaming God. Life is full of circumstances that force growth amid mistakes, fear, heartache, and self-doubt. This book aims to provide you with solid footing within these complex feelings, inviting you to embrace failure as a stepping stone to growth, make hard choices in the face of uncertainty, reach for God's outstretched hand even when it feels like he's not listening, and ultimately emerge victorious.

Come with me on this journey, where you'll glean insights to lead with greater confidence, navigate life's uncertainties with clarity, and resiliently bounce back from its unforeseen turns. Whether you find yourself scaling professional mountains, navigating personal valleys, or weathering unforeseen crises, I want you to know reclaiming control is about understanding and seeing that God is with you in the chaos. Right as everything is falling apart, through it all he is ready to you help bounce back. You have the capacity to reclaim the driver's seat of your life.

Let's be honest—life has a way of surprising us. Unexpected plot twists can feel like a two-by-four to the face. This conversation about faith, failure, and how we keep moving forward when everything is falling apart is meant to equip you for the fight in front of you. The goal is to live intentionally, reclaim hope with strength and courage, and trust in God's commitment to you.

This journey we're on together is about you snatching back what's rightfully yours. Whatever you've handed over, those places you feel unsteady, I'm here to build you up so you can reclaim it all. Instead of offering comfort from a place of detachment, I share true stories that expose the tensions we all face, leaving you to decide how they fit into your life. I am offering hope and tools to help you bounce back and gain perspective. These stories span over two decades, are not in chronological order, and the names have been changed for privacy.

By the last page, you'll have the courage to stand with your back straight and your face forward. Recognizing just how present God is in your story and your ability to persevere no matter what awaits you. No more excuses, no more fear holding you back. We are no longer looking at our feet. Today, we begin building a bridge toward better.

You've already come so far, and your potential knows no bounds. With God by your side, neither mistakes nor regret can cast shadows over your faith.

Remember, I once prayed for rain to wash away my burdens, memories, and blemishes of failure. Fortunately, it did not deliver.

ONE

SPLINTERED HOPE

WILL YOUR ANCHOR HOLD?

I have been called a "token" many times in my career. This term is used in corporate settings to say a person, usually a minority, has been invited, hired, or promoted only because of their gender or the color of their skin, rather than their skills or intellect.

Most professional women can list off several controversial phrases tossed in their direction while walking through long echoey hallways of businesses, academic buildings, or even within Christian ministries. Often, I would hear about these comments secondhand or under the cowardly mumble of a colleague after a disagreement, the words barely audible over the sound of their frustrated footsteps grating heavily against the carpet.

However, never had someone scheduled a meeting to call me a "token" to my face. That is, not until my promotion. I knew certain people would not be happy about the leadership decision. Days prior, I stood in my driveway, freezing, as I prepared myself for the onslaught of distrust, skepticism, and second-guessing. This had nothing to do with imposter syndrome. I knew I had earned everything being offered to me. I also deeply desired to be wrong about what I anticipated would happen after the announcement.

As I sat in my office chair, the large glass wall allowed the sunlight to tightly hug the fibers of my suit jacket, wrapping me in the invisible embrace I needed. My colleague made his presence known in front of the oak door and entered. His face was relaxed, but his eyes were blazing telling me everything I needed to know before he even uttered a word.

What I have come to realize—a lesson that would continue to be validated and refined in the years to come—is this: misplaced hope ushers us toward frantic living, unhealthy dependency, and a life built on and sustained by comparison.

I had this in mind when I faced, yet again, another mistake looking back at me. I had made a habit of placing trust in those I worked with, believing we would all look out for each other at the peaks in the same way we did in the valleys. However, over the years, power, money, and access shattered my preconceived notions. Access was revealing itself to be about more than mere proximity to certain resources. It transcended physical boundaries, delving deeper into networks, opportunities, and realms of influence, now synonymous with the currency of connectivity and control. This particular conversation would bring all these facets to the surface.

My colleague knew nothing of my mental turmoil or the personal load I was carrying. I did not expect him to care as I waved him in to sit. He likely would have found it amusing knowing I had deliberately walked into nature's white noise expecting answers, a decision made by someone who had already played Russian roulette with their confidence several times prior, each choice carrying the potential to dismantle the fragile armor of self-assurance I had painstakingly constructed.

Although I thought I was prepared for the conversation, I was once again shocked by how quickly a relationship can change. This is the painful reality of trusting the wrong individuals, especially when their true motives are laid to bare under the glaring spotlight of success and "more." I would again find myself rattled, this time needing to rebound even quicker as our relationship shifted from the moment he opened his mouth. In the days to come I would learn that the fracturing had begun months prior.

"Bethny, I'm going to be honest. You are a token promotion. Most of what you have received [the awards] is because you are Black, a woman, and attractive."

I blinked, my face refusing to show the disgust and wave of anger wanting to make an appearance. As he continued, I simply wondered where he found the gall to speak to his new boss with such confidence, as if there would be no repercussions for such a poor choice of words.

He continued by explaining in detail how our leaders and the board had gotten the promotion wrong, how I was undeserving because of my age and time with the company. He discounted my extensive résumé and the more than five years we had worked alongside each other before this dreadful conversation.

As he reached his conclusion, I put aside the fear regarding my ability to lead a team spread across the globe. I silenced all the echoes discounting my worth. I put the pain of another broken relationship in the back of my mind and thanked him for his time.

I looked forward, even though internally I wrestled with the lies and doubts.

My mentor, Denise, taught me to move in silence, while my father had taught me the importance of never allowing my emotions to have the final say. Though appearing composed and prepared, I was, in fact, unsteady. Everything was falling apart. In the coming weeks, I would question if God had opened this door for me, my colleague would exit the organization, and we would never speak again.

BEGGING AND BORROWING

While this chapter isn't about audacity, let's take a moment to acknowledge a prevailing truth: some people have a lot of audacity and can weaponize it to cut others to pieces. No matter where you find yourself in life, consider these fundamental truths:

You do not have to conform to the audacity others present to you.

You do not have to acknowledge disrespect.

You do not have to defend what God has already decided.

The question we are faced with repeatedly, the one I asked myself after my colleague closed the office door as he exited, is, Why and how did I get here?

Why and how do we repeatedly find ourselves in situations where we justify bending to the point of fracturing our core? Why do we end up in relationships that cause distraction and internal withering, making us unrecognizable to ourselves? Then the pursuit of God becomes a desperate search, leaving us off-balance and questioning our ability to move forward with power.

It's abnormal to be satisfied with scrambling for validation, surface support, or momentary waves of relief. Standing still, contemplating if God opened the door only to abandon us upon entry should not be common. Such behavior is not a part of his character or nature. When we shift our gaze away from God, we create the perfect entry point for mistrust.

As my colleague left my office, I sat there wrestling with his opinions because I had invested significant time and energy in our relationship and had high expectations for it. The question persists: How do we keep arriving at these places? Enter stage left what I call the "splintering of hope." This is when we borrow parts of God's promises and truths, then entrust the execution and outcome of these promises to the care of those around us.

While it's logical to put confidence in others, that decision can prove costly if our focus changes. We misstep when we figuratively push God to the back seat, allowing his words to become faint and the noise of others to overtake our thoughts. We welcome dismay when God is no longer a consideration in the present or future steps we take.

Here, we are often left disappointed and confused because we forget that people, no matter their intentions, often aren't consistently reliable because life happens to us all. Lowering our expectations becomes a natural response, and in the fog of it all, we forget that no person is meant to do what is intended to be done by God alone. When our hope and trust become bound to how people feel about us, we are left exposed in ways we cannot fathom. Psalm 118:8 tells us, "It is better to take refuge in the LORD than to trust in humans." It's a simple yet powerful verse.

What may seem like momentary steps away from our center can create a shift in our foundation. Suddenly, God is not our only refuge, at least not one we're satisfied with. The mind races toward a new narrative: God needs the help of those in positions of power or influence to propel us forward. Success now depends on someone else's access, not God's promises. But the truth is that God is not dependent on anyone. Placing our full trust in him and making decisions with him will always be the safest place our hope can rest.

I fell into the slippery trap of believing I needed certain relationships to maintain my success and overcome obstacles because I had begun looking at God through the rearview mirror. I wasn't focusing on how these relationships required me to make significant compromises. I bought into the lie that likability within office dynamics was the only way to win. "If people don't like me, I can't be successful," I thought, as if "likability" and social status aren't as vulnerable as the breeze. This line of thinking left me repeatedly disappointed and isolated.

We parcel off our hope as though it is a commodity, as if our heart swelling with anticipation of what could be is not precious or deserving of care. But there is a cost to where we put our focus, which is why corporations invest billions to have it.

The misplacement of my hope and the darting of my gaze made my dependency on labels, titles, competition, and arbitrary goals significantly easier. It also left me questioning why God was "taking his time" answering prayers and removing barriers. I was walking an emotional tightrope long before that conversation with my colleague. His words were just another blow.

Let me be clear about something: Forming a professional bond is not the issue. Nor is trusting friends and family over the natural evolution of a relationship. We should have confidence in people and seek wisdom within our ambition or the execution of our dreams. The failure lies in believing that we need man's acknowledgment over and before God's. This is when our hope splinters, making us vulnerable and our thoughts clouded.

When I planted my feet on unsteady ground and attached my hope to people and things that couldn't withstand the storms around me, I crumbled. The words of my colleague landed hard.

His lack of belief in my abilities made me question my proficiency.

His matter-of-fact approach caused me to pause.

His disgust for a Black woman in leadership made me suddenly question my influence.

We assume that when the chaos comes, we will be able to flip a switch and our dusty faith will jump several gears, immediately fixing our problems. This is not how it works. God is the God of relationship for a reason. Though he is always present, he is not a genie to be called upon only when our version of "comfort" is no longer satisfying. He is the living God who desires to walk through all the mess with you. Unknowingly, I had handed over my confidence when I needed it most and found myself questioning whether God had really opened the door. With the promotion, I faced new levels of fear and pressure, greater hurdles, and different types of mental and emotional waves.

When we parcel off what is precious and meant only for God, at some point we must come to terms with that decision. Even when God kicks the door off its hinges, entrusting the wrong people with our vision, confidence, and faith will lead us down dark roads.

COMPARISON

Comparison is a relentless force that often leads us to justify poor decisions and gamble with authenticity. It is an extreme sport, a colorless and odorless fuel, that, if not managed properly, inflicts damage on all who participate.

In a strategy meeting with entrepreneurs, I emphasized the dangers of using the lens of comparison to decide whether something is lacking within us. Doing so is an open invitation for shame to weave into the fabric of our being, which creates an unexpected power imbalance when we hand ourselves over to opinions of others.

When we play games with our identity and hope, what once felt like a solid foundation becomes irrelevant and mundane. Deep disappointment sets in, souring the progress we were once satisfied with. Suddenly, we're no longer good enough, and God's promises lose their timeliness and sufficiency. The support of friends tilts toward "they don't understand" as we find reasons to move away from what was once steady progress.

Comparison is a fun house full of mirrors where nothing appears as it really is and truth remains elusive. This best kept secret has most of us leaving the fun house worse than we were before. Yet we continue to go back in with every scroll, post, click, and mummer. Each round of this silent game empowers the illusions and lies, leading to more distorted perspectives.

The combination of comparison and competition emboldened my colleague to make disparaging remarks about my success, my misplaced hope from years prior fueled my internal struggle.

It's difficult to admit that we can so easily fall

into the trap of comparison and also place so much hope in others, but it's crucial to discuss anything that causes us to devalue ourselves and God. Handing over parts of our faith or hope for short-term gain can come at a significant cost. The questions arise: What are you willing to do to be seen? Is playing this comparison game and sacrificing parts of your faith or hope worth it?

Here is a different question: Are you willing to crush another person or allow them to do the same to you? The fun house's distortion aims to knock you off-balance, providing an unsustainable motivator that won't enrich your life. Instead, it propels you to look toward others for refuge, validation, and purpose, leaving your open hands still half empty.

The alternative, though not simple, is freeing. It requires commitment and a willingness to stop turning your head left and right when feeling hopeless or alone. You will never find true refuge in people, because humans are prone to failure. Put aside envy and ego, and decide to live life outside the grip of external validation.

It's time to stop tiptoeing around a subject that cripples forward movement and creates identity issues. The chase of comparison is endless, with no real benefit for the winner or the loser. People aren't corporations or sporting entities, whose data can be compared and analyzed in a straightforward manner. Instead, we are intricate beings with emotions and vulnerabilities. That's why toxic behaviors attached to comparison lead to so much disappointment, shame, and reckless behavior.

The bottom of this barrel involves justifying actions that require shortchanging and disrespecting another person. It places a person in the seat of "I am better than them" and "I deserve this no matter the cost," making anything fair game, even calling someone a "token" to their face.

There's a fine line between comparing to improve and comparing to the detriment of another person. Choose wisely. Once your hope splinters, you lose control, and are weakened under the weight of pride and regret. I know from experience. I once made choices to advance in my career by conforming, going silent, and looking the other way in the face of office politics. This is where misplaced hope and comparison pushed me, away from my center and to the receiving end of words meant to break me. Where will decisions like this take you?

LOST FOOTING

Comparison is not the only reason we may find ourselves splintering our hope. Toxic dependency when leading, both personally and professionally, is something else we have to watch out for. No matter the space, this dependency on others impacts decision-making. It creates dynamics where we trust ourselves a little less. It causes us to stutter-step during execution and over time has us listening to the wrong people in the name of "politics," self-soothing, or quick solutions.

Seeking approval in shallow waters has left its mark on my life—grayed my hair, created stomach issues, and given me a persistent sense of diminished worth. Though seeking input can be wise in decision-making, losing sight of where others' thoughts and opinions belong can lead to seeking validation to the point of stagnation or compromising our steps to appease the majority.

By the time I was promoted to the position of senior vice president, I had unwittingly fractured parts of my identity, altering the core of what I believed. This influenced both professional and personal choices as my worth became tethered to the promises of people. It was as if I were looking at myself through an altered lens.

Our misstep occurs when we transition from seeking perspective and wisdom to excessively relying on people's opinions and advice, making decisions based on the feelings of others instead of our rightfully placed desires. The end goal can be lost to overcompromise, and even the voice of God can become muffled in the clamor of external influences.

This suggestion is not rooted in distrusting people but recognizing when we've placed more weight on the words and actions of others rather than on God. While we may often give God credit for opened doors and blessings, we can find ourselves in states of desperation or agitation when the attitudes of others don't align with our real intentions or goals.

The promises and declarations of others can never serve as reliable anchors. Clinging tightly to the applause, validation, and approval of peers, leaders, and influencers will inevitably leave us floating in a sea of choppy waters, with nothing solid to hold on to. In such turbulent times, the pivotal question surfaces: Will your anchor hold in the face of challenges?

The question not only tests the strength of our convictions but also dictates where we turn to regain stability, focus, or reconnection with ourselves. If God isn't an integral part of your firm foundation, it's time to initiate that change today.

Your anchor travels with you, whether in calm or stormy seas. Rather than changing with the seasons, you can be grounded enough to weather storms and bask in the sun's brightest rays. Other people don't make good anchors because undeniably:

Opinions change, sometimes not in our favor.

People transition out of our lives for many reasons.

People mature and change as the years teach us new lessons and bring reminders of old missteps.

So the anchor you choose throughout life is pivotal. Reflect on instances when you've not stood on solid ground and you'll probably discover that, in those moments, your hope weakened. Perhaps, like me, you ventured into questioning God amid the turbulence of internal emotions, unrealized circumstances, thoughts distorted by the lens of comparison, and notions of entitlement. Let today be the day this stops. Ground yourself in an unshakable hope that transcends the fickle winds of external influences.

REFUGE

Let this resonate as your rallying cry: God's hands remain the safest space for your faith, hope, and vision. Toxic comparison finds no refuge there. It's a sanctuary to which you can always retreat when the shadows of comparison loom. In the grand tapestry of your heart and mind, no one should ever supersede God's position. I don't care who they are.

Your hope is not some circumstantial savior, arriving only on days of crisis. It is with you always. If your anchor is Christ, if your hope rests in him, it will endure. He walks with you in the cool of the day and cradles you in desperation, unwavering against the fiercest storms, toxic words, or gravest mistakes.

In the face of setbacks or failure, we often revisit old notes. Yet not every lesson is meant to be carried forward or paraded as a post. Liberate yourself from the burden of expecting remnants of old to carry you through new chapters. Start new, today. Right now.

If you do, shady advice will lose its allure, now a mere distraction. No longer will you halfway trust God; you'll surrender every situation and circumstance to him. Cease attaching fragments of your hope to that which is changeable, inconsistent, and unpredictable. Stop running everyone else's race;

there's no satisfaction for you there. Once you recognize that running someone else's race, no matter their level of success, leads to mediocrity, you will begin to stride through life with renewed purpose.

When compromise beckons at your door, recognize there is a decision to be made—and remember, you are the decision-maker. Shift your gaze back to the Word of God, forsaking those hollow promises made to appease in the moment and words that merely stroke your ego. To ease internal agitation, trust him rather than leaning even slightly on your own understanding or that of others. God beckons us to trust him fully because he cares deeply and knows all. This is in our favor because God moves at a winning pace. Despite our disappointment, setbacks, and frustrations, he reigns above time, unbound by its constraints. Lean on him, set your focus, and forsake the fun house of mirrors called comparison. Turn your attention toward the beauty that is his refuge—the place where, even when we feel unsteady, hope, strength, and faith flourish.

TWO

HURDLES
OVERCOMING

Life throws many hurdles at us. When we face challenges (some lasting for months or even years), we sometimes doubt who we are and what we stand for. As we question our abilities, it can be easy to find ourselves so overwhelmed or paralyzed by self-doubt that we stop moving forward altogether.

I remember one business trip rather vividly—a trip where I encountered three major hurdles connected to knowing who I am, where I belong, and my own worth. During this trip I was reminded of what happens when self-doubt is not swiftly wrestled to the ground, suffocated, and left for dead. It was yet another situation where I was forced to reckon with what happens when we seek validation from others—and the unseen consequences that follow.

After landing in Oregon, the executive team I was traveling with made its way to the Duniway hotel. Being a classic introvert, I wandered away from my colleagues and over to the hotel's boutique coffee stand as we waited for our rooms. I ordered the hazelnut latte. It was perfect, just as advertised. Soon we were making our way to the elevators as I sipped a coffee so delightful that it reminded me of everything good in life.

As usual we had a short window of time to change from our casual traveling clothes to business attire. In one clumsy swoop, I swapped out my black tights and loose-fitting shirt with a black dress. My comfortable shoes shifted quickly into silver stiletto heels. My big curls covered any facial imperfections, and red lipstick would be all the makeup I needed in the Pacific Northwest sun. With minutes to spare, I headed back down to the lobby and ordered a second cup of coffee. The time change was already dancing across my eyelids, and the business trip had barely begun. I would be tired within a matter of hours.

As I turned to join the team, I heard words I have encountered throughout my career: "Who invited you?" The question from the fellow executive was ridiculous given that we had just flown together across the country on a private plane. But no matter how absurd the question, it still triggered the first hurdle: feeling rejected. But he wasn't done. "I don't even know why we need you here . . ." Hurdle two: doubt.

Bullying never really stops. It lives on beyond middle school and college years. It follows us into our careers, adult friendships, and onto newly formed playgrounds such as dinner parties, social events, and online platforms. It does not matter how much money, power, or privilege we obtain; an intimidator is always lurking in the shadows. Boundaries in the workplace may reduce open disrespect, but they by no means eliminate it or shield anyone completely.

My back went straight, my spine becoming so solid it felt like dried cement. My hair's naturally blond, red, and brown hues became air cover, helping deflect the burning irritation slicing through me. He dragged on for a few more seconds, but it felt like hours. To top it all off, he spoke every word within earshot of my team, other executives, and the hotel staff. But no one spoke up to defend me. "Am I not worth getting in the ring for?" I wondered. Ah, there it was, hurdle three: feeling worthless.

I didn't blink. My heart raced as I breathed without actually taking in enough oxygen to pace my thoughts. I wanted to clench my fists, but the gesture would be too obvious, a clear signal of frustration. So I sipped the best hazelnut coffee I have ever had, smiled, and replied, "Well, I guess you are about to find out."

Humor and stoic composure have always been swords I could wield when caught flat-footed. But inside, I was stressed, perplexed, and angry. I wished I had read my Bible the previous night as my mind searched for a calming verse from the book of Proverbs. Nothing came to mind. But the effort of scrambling for solid footing was the cue I needed to bite my tongue as anger attempted to storm above the surface. This man was a living, breathing bully who desired to minimize me.

My mouth went dry, and my jaw straightened as I attempted to bore into him with my whiskey-colored eyes. He stared back at me, waiting for a more detailed response. I said nothing.

Sometimes we must allow silence to do the work. We must give God room to step in and allow interactions to be cut short before anything escalates beyond our control. In other instances, we remain silent because no response is warranted.

Frustrated with my lack of engagement, he turned his thin lips down and gave a disapproving grunt echoing from his gut. Then he slowly marched away. I stood, smiling hard, giving the impression of confidence and unbotheredness. Inside I felt invalidated. Worthless. Small. All the doubts I thought were hidden away or under control were now wide awake. *Did he know something I didn't know? Was he in on some secret?* I dared not validate any of these questions out loud with words or actions. He had unknowingly breathed life into things I thought were dead.

My boss exited the elevator with a big smile, and we walked with the rest of the team toward the black luxury cars lining the front of the hotel sidewalk. As the warm leather and minty fragrance of the car's interior grabbed my senses, my eyes focused on the skyline. I sat in silence, chewing the inside of my bottom lip and thinking through all the what-ifs. Old hurdles had returned, and this time I hadn't cleared one. And the truth of this crushed me.

A SOLID FOUNDATION

Learning to overcome life's hurdles is a process. I have been on this planet for over forty years and realize that the three hurdles I struggled with on that business trip—doubt, belonging, and worth—cause a lot of us to question our value and abilities.

Though each hurdle is different, together, they can quickly become intertwined and distort what we see in our reflection, making them a paralyzing combination. In subtle or overt ways, we are challenged with defending, analyzing, or questioning three things simultaneously:

1. Who am I?
2. Do I belong?
3. Who decides my worth?

These three questions don't always come up at the most convenient times. They surface during hectic moments at home, in business meetings, during carpools, or when scrolling online. When we are too tired to think, we unknowingly begin looking to others to answer these questions on our behalf: Who am I? Do I belong? Who decides my worth?

If we lack experience or knowledge, it can appear easier to depend on those who have gone before us for direction and clarity. We rarely divert away from the footsteps previously made, because the direction seems right. "If it worked for them, it would probably provide me with a similar outcome," we think.

We take personality tests, read articles, and listen to podcasts to answer or solidify the answers to these three questions. Which is perfectly fine. But it's a mistake to allow others significant buy-in regarding the answers to these questions. No one should answer on your behalf. And handing over this type of power to others almost always guarantees that self-worth will become a repeated hurdle.

Anytime we parcel off worth, we will eventually find ourselves feeling off-balance. To remain secure and balanced, you must know your own worth. You must know that you know that you know! If you divide your worth or value into pieces and parts, allowing others to define it for you, you lose fragments of yourself. You hand over things never meant to leave your grasp.

In some cases, this impact is deeper than splintering hope because it allows others to decide the fundamentals of who you are, with your permission and on your behalf.

This world is overflowing with advice, wisdom, courses, and masterminds. But none of it will sustain you over the long haul if you can't answer these three questions yourself. And even when advice is dripping with wisdom, it may not apply to your situation or circumstance. I am not saying tools aren't beneficial.

I am a student of life. I graduated at the top of my university class and have gone on to serve on academic boards, join prestigious leadership academies, and rub shoulders with some of the most educated individuals and public officials in our country. Yet until I could answer these questions for myself, I struggled to bounce back after disappointment. It didn't matter who I was in the room with or what I knew on an intellectual level, I still felt empty.

One thing I have been reminded of repeatedly. It's something I carry with me even when sitting on the corner of the couch talking with my friends about day-to-day life. It's this: We aren't meant to shoulder the burden of other people's realities forever. We were not born to impress the masses. We aren't meant to take someone else's story and make it our story.

We can't be bold and courageous without solidifying the foundation—what our feet stand on in the peaks and valleys. A solid foundation is paramount to reclaiming hope after being knocked off-balance and maintaining a gritty resilience when stuck in the trenches. We must each know, deep within the marrow of our bones, who we are and what we stand for.

This certainty will keep you grounded in life's storms. It will guide you out of the chaos without having to survive by leaning on someone else's victory

or story. Your answers to these three questions—
Who am I? Do I belong? Who decides my worth?
—is the foundation needed to overcome the hurdles
you are facing.

WHO AM I?

In case no one has told you, understanding yourself
takes time, continually evolving as you experience
different aspects of life and enter new seasons. That
lobby encounter wasn't the first time I had failed
to clear hurdles related to doubt, worthlessness,
and rejection, and it certainly wouldn't be my last.
Like me, you will find yourself wrestling with these
hurdles time and again, each instance demanding a
fresh commitment. There is no quick fix. You must
decide over and over who you are, what is important to you, adapting to the ebb and flow of life's
circumstances. And when self-doubt attempts to
make an appearance, you will need to lean into the
unwavering goodness of God.

When rattled after the door has been slammed in
your face, and the ache feels too great, even then, you
can look to the heavens and know that "all things
work together for the good of those who love him,

who have been called according to his purpose" (Romans 8:28). This verse still applies to you even when the circumstances seem to imply that God has left this part of your story. Keep in mind: It is only through God that we find the certainty necessary to surmount obstacles and experience sustainable personal growth.

Self-doubt—which is a smooth arc toward fear—attempts to keep us trapped on thin ice. It surrounds us with such a deep feeling of uncertainty that we become overwhelmed by the dread of stepping forward, speaking up, or falling through the cracks. Once doubt has taken hold, it strips away our exterior, leaving us bare. All we can see are contradictions and questions. We mistrust God, his Word, and truth.

When doubt is present, it suffocates us until we can no longer think about moving beyond the point of impact. Maybe Romans 8:28 was a once familiar Scripture, but now it seems like a distant concept that no longer applies to you. God's Word has become circumstantial in your mind, and this deadly spiral can be hard to unwind.

Knowing who you are before people try to decide that for you is your greatest defense against self-doubt. Knowing who you are in Christ is your most potent weapon against feelings of worthlessness or being unwanted.

Proverbs 3:5–8 (ESV) remains significant to me in these moments of struggle:

> Trust in the LORD with all your heart,
>   and do not lean on your own
>   understanding.
> In all your ways acknowledge him,
>   and he will make straight your paths.
> Be not wise in your own eyes;
>   fear the LORD, and turn away from evil.
> It will be healing to your flesh
>   and refreshment to your bones.

This is not a soft verse. This is where we gain certainty when worthlessness on the job or in relationships enters the conversation. This is how we find the strength to move forward and stand with our backs straight in the middle of the storm. It's how we keep moments of doubt from becoming lasting imprints within our hearts and minds.

With God, you are a force to be reckoned with. When you involve him in the answers connected to questions of who you are, you build on a firm foundation that will not give way, allowing you to return to the center of who you really are. So, who are you? Whether you are new to your faith or seasoned, you will face countless storms in this life. To keep overcoming, to reclaim hope repeatedly, you must have confidence in God's unwavering assurance as his child. Believe that he will not be pushed aside by the chaos you are facing or the doubts in your mind.

You are forgiven, you are called, and a cherished child of God. This affirmation is grounded in truths that surpass our doubts. You are what your faith is attached to and the power working within you.

Remember this: Only God can bring the level of certainty we need to overcome obstacles and grow. He is the perfect cornerstone for whatever you are building toward or coming out of. So, whoever you are, engrave Proverbs 3:5–8 on your heart and mind. And decide to walk in the confidence of knowing who you are in Christ, which is not dependent on the validation or approval of others.

DO I BELONG?

When we feel unwanted, it means a part of us has a desire to belong. I once yearned for someone to acknowledge that I belonged in certain rooms without me having to justifying my presence. No matter the number of awards or amount of confidence from my community, I desired a nod from people who were not *my* people.

Surface approval can overshadow what we deem important and influence how we view ourselves Even Bible verses like Isaiah 43:4 (ESV), "You are precious in my eyes," don't always prevent us from seeking final approval outside of God's love. But, as we discussed previously, when we do this, our hope splinters and we place what is precious into unfit hands.

This desire for belonging within the communities in which we live, work, or serve is natural. Yet admitting this may cause some of us to tense up as we consider someone saying, "Eh, you aren't good enough." We vacillate between wanting to belong and being afraid of potential rejection, making small compromises along the way as we water down who we are in an effort to feel connected.

There is a beautiful quote by Brené Brown in her book *Braving the Wilderness*: "True belonging doesn't require you to change who you are; it requires you to be who you are."[1] When I first read these

---

1. Brené Brown, *Braving the Wilderness: The Quest for True Belonging and the Courage to Stand Alone* (New York: Random House, 2017), 40.

words, I was making my way through a crowded airport. The statement leaped toward me because I was actively doing the opposite. At that point, I was willing to change myself and encouraged others to do the same in the spirit of "community" and office politics. I forced myself into spaces and places because I believed my worth was hidden there or that people would recognize my value once I arrived. I allowed others to have the final say regarding who I was and found ways to justify the small compromises.

The desire to belong places us, at times, in the wrong rooms. We find ourselves in spaces and relationships God is actively attempting to shield us from. Not because we are undeserving or deemed "better" than other people but because those spaces or people aren't intended for us.

To help keep the desire for belonging in its proper place, try embracing this concept: You aren't meant to appeal to every person or created to fit into every space. When we connect our desire to belong with the wrong people, it can send us right back to the starting blocks of self-doubt. When we change the core of who we are for temporary approval, it opens the door to feelings of worthlessness.

Remember, knowing who I am, where I belong, and my own worth are different issues that are deeply intertwined. We can make better decisions regarding belonging and the spaces we choose to enter by adding the following to how we approach our day-to-day: Fully understand and embrace your purpose in Christ. Build community rooted in authenticity, not simply surface support. And proactively decide not to contort who you are to fit in.

Walk boldly and in confidence. Even if there are seasons when it is only you and God. The right people, relationships, and business partners will come in time. Do not settle; cherish this time.

WHO DECIDES MY WORTH?

Several years ago, I found myself in a meeting with an executive—an esteemed member of the organization, highly respected, and known for clear thinking and quick conclusions. On this particular day, however, something was amiss. His usual confidence was overshadowed by a struggle to articulate his thoughts, a distraction that seemed unrelated to work.

As he spoke, I stood up, walked to the window, and asked, "What is happening here?" He paused, likely weighing how to respond. We had developed a mutual respect for each other, so the question wasn't off base. Then the successful father of four, with a beautiful wife I deeply adored, firmly stated, "I still feel like I can't get anything right, Bethny. No matter what I do."

This conversation unveiled what I now term "sticky weights"—lingering negative words and thoughts that we struggle to release. They follow us even as we reach significant milestones or goals. It isn't easy to let go of words or actions that minimize us in any capacity. When certain statements are repeated back to you often and frequently, they become a part of your internal vocabulary. Soon these sticky weights are part of the burden we carry, affecting how we live and move in the world.

My coworker shared insecurities dating back to college that continued to haunt him, each new accomplishment accompanied by the burden of past negativities. The relentless drive to prove others wrong, though a powerful force, proved unsustainable for prolonged periods. Confidence, satisfaction, and peace waver when feelings of worthlessness hold even a small part of the narrative.

Because I've grappled with similar struggles, my heart empathized with my colleague. I observed a common theme as he spoke about challenges that money, power, or community couldn't ease.

I recognized myself and countless others in his words. Yet this was a workplace setting, and the focus was on his struggles, not mine. So I posed a simple question that I now extend to you: *Who decides your worth?*

This is a drum worth beating. Who you allow to make ongoing deposits into your heart, mind, and spirit impacts what you see in the mirror and the value you think you bring to certain spaces.

When considering who influences your self-worth, it's important to set sturdy boundaries around your sense of value. Be purposeful in choosing whose voices carry weight in your life, deciding on the front end who gets input. Seek out those who consistently respect and uplift you, regardless of the circumstances. Of course, you should remain open to feedback and understand other perspectives for personal growth; this is how we learn and mature. But no one's thoughts should supersede the truth you carry deep within the marrow of your bones. You determine which opinions, views, and perspectives matter the most.

Before we move forward, take a moment to consider those who you allow to help shape your view of your own worth and value. Then ask yourself: Do they align with what God has told you about yourself? Have you positioned them above your own internal voice? And are they contributing positively to your sense of self-worth and value? Learn from my mistakes, and don't seek answers in the wrong places.

ONWARD

When I returned to my hotel room after being disregarded, overlooked, and bullied, I stared at myself in the mirror. There she was once again—a woman rejected, expected to perform, tired of pretending, and broken into fragments.

That night, I tossed and turned in my sleep, engaged in a wrestling match with God, trying to rationalize the truth with what I was facing. I had come this far in life, yet once again found myself feeling unsteady on my feet when facing familiar giants, those nemeses I thought I had defeated and left behind. Perhaps you've wrestled with God in a similar manner, questioning if there's something inherently wrong with you or if your life's burden is to be perpetually suffocated.

For the most part, I now clear these three hurdles quicker. By leaning on my faith and finding strength in God's unwavering assurance, I have built up a resilience over the years. By refusing to let fear dictate my decisions even as things are crumbling around me and anchoring myself in the truth of my identity in Christ, even when I fall flat on my face, I find myself getting back up with a renewed sense and a burning desire to start again. Maybe not immediately, but in time. By putting what I have shared with you into practice, I am not so easily rattled and rarely knocked off-balance in such a way that I question the core of who I am. This is the power of embracing failure and applying my faith to any life lessons. But do not be fooled. I still have moments of doubt, and the sting of rejection finds me on occasion. At times fear chases me as a form of entertainment, using others as a mouthpiece to amplify untruths.

While writing this book, I found myself weeping beside a rotten tree on a solo hike in the Colorado mountains, confronted with new hurdles. But I felt as though God took his finger, placed it under my trembling chin, and tenderly reminded me to keep my eyes on him. This reassurance and comfort found me quicker than it had in previous years.

Obstacles had not vanished; they awaited me at the bottom of that mountain. Yet knowing who I am and who loves me allowed for a faster return to solid ground. The same can be true for you. The next time you feel uncertain, pause on these points:

1. Know who you are before people decide for you.
2. Understand who you are before considering the opinions of others. True belonging doesn't require you to change who you are.
3. Decide that what you and God say about your worth matters most.

As you implement these lessons into your life, embedding them into your thought patterns, remember this: When hurdles arise, keep taking steps forward, even if they're shaky. Refuse to let fear dictate your decisions. Don't allow sticky weights to drag you down. While overcoming these hurdles is possible, it requires your courage to confront them head-on. Remember, as you move forward, working to reclaim hope with each step, reflect on the three questions posed in this chapter. May you embrace the truth that you are a child of God, you belong, and you are of immeasurable worth.

THREE

WHITE-KNUCKLED

RESOLUTE

It was cold and rainy as I pulled the car into my driveway. Leaves covered most of the blacktop, an array of burnt orange, red, and faded green paving the way toward the entry. I did not have the energy to open the heavy front door. There was nothing but responsibility on the other side. Another argument brewing beneath the surface. Another late night of work calls, emails, and hidden anxiety.

I parked the car at the top of the driveway and sat. I was attempting to hide from my life behind the giant oak trees with their long branches stretching toward heaven.

There is something about sitting alone in a car that evokes deep feelings. Emotions from the day labored to be acknowledged, and I actively worked to keep them in place until it was safe to let them surface. But if I sat long enough, I was bound to be overcome by them.

To avoid this, I started counting the raindrops as they hit the sunroof. The rain's calming rhythm made me wonder if God would reach down and give me a cocoon-like embrace, allowing me to finally unfold in a way I had not been able to in years. The taps reminded me of my cadence when I run: *Heel, toe, heel, toe, heel, toe. Not too fast, not too slow.*

Lately, I had been terribly overwhelmed, feeling unprepared as I moved from one moment to the next. I seemingly did it all with such ease that no one knew I was barely keeping my head above water, going from obstacle to obstacle, feeling to feeling.

I looked at my passenger seat: unopened bills, spreadsheets, and business proposals needing my approval. As my eyes returned to the dancing rain, I wondered when all this would catch up with me. Every step seemed to take more of my breath away. I had long forgotten how to breathe with intentionality. Here I was holding in one hand what I had prayed for—vibrant children, a flourishing career marked by success beyond measure, unparalleled access to opportunities I had never dreamed of. It was clear

God's fingerprints were on my life. Then in the other hand, turmoil.

I couldn't see beyond what was in front of me. All I saw were patterns of failure, big and small. Sacrifice, loneliness, and unmet expectations. I sat wishing open doors had remained closed. I wished myself different. I wondered why I remained sure God was pushing me forward but simultaneously felt so miserable.

A cloud of loneliness had me frozen in that car, not wanting to enter my house. Disappointment created self-imposed distance between me and God. I needed some type of burning bush because I wasn't sure how much longer I could survive on leaps of faith. As I sat listening to the rain, silently praying for answers, I became even more overwhelmed by the valley that had transformed into trench living.

My teeth rattled from the tension my body held, forcing me to put the car in drive due to the discomfort and my brain's refusal to settle, yet I kept my foot on the brake. I felt unmovable while internally I coiled around myself. I did not want to move. I was searching for the God in my present story while sitting white-knuckled and with clenched teeth in my driveway.

The longer I sat, the tighter my fists gripped the wheel. Finally, the pressure caused pain to shoot through my fingers, jump-starting my thinking.

"What is the point of all this anymore? How much longer can I keep up the facade?" I would get no answers. Plus, another headache was on the way.

What happened to my life?

WHEN DREAMS MORPH

What happened?

How many times have you sat in the car, stood in the kitchen or garage, stared out a window, and asked yourself this very question?

No one plans for their path to take a turn into uncharted waters. No one really expects the bottom to drop from beneath our feet midstride. We walk through life fully expectant, with plans and hope as we carry forward the lessons from yesterday into new jobs, parenting, friendships, marriage, or the budding of newly developing relationships. With time, we attach dreams and laughter to the people we want to experience joy with. We pray and ask God to help open doors as we work toward making those dreams a reality.

But what happens when the dreams morph after we have walked through the door God opened? What happens when the plans and strategies need to change due to unforeseen circumstances? Does this mean we got it wrong? Does it mean we were blind and mishandled something? What happens when hope becomes heavy, the belief in what should be begins weighing us down in the present, soon allowing circumstances to distort how we see God? Where do we turn when the questions take us down dark roads with even fewer answers than before?

These tough questions are a very real reality. Some of us face them over time, but some of us have seasons when we are hit with their compounding effect all at once. No matter how we envision life after we've reached the goal, held the dream, or experienced an answered prayer, life keeps right on changing—and sometimes our desires need to morph too. How do we reclaim hope? How do we maintain optimism when the happiness we thought would sustain us becomes unsettled?

Few things unfold in the way we envisioned. This type of change can rattle anyone. But the fear can be especially intense in certain situations. Trepidation shows its face when we are leading, going deeper into relationships, starting again, or ending things we have held on to for ages. It attempts to overshadow our progress, delight, or the clarity in the answers we seek. Fear, worry, regret, and failure cloud every possibility.

We're left in profound contemplation, almost immobile, as we see flashes of the path ahead. Recognizing the next steps may mean facing significant obstacles and, at times, enduring heartaches as we stumble forward. We have to overcome yet another hurdle, attempt once again to heal and become whole.

It is in these moments we realize it takes a little bit of crazy to keep finding the strength to continue pressing forward again and again. This is why the first step is not always the hardest one. Yes, it is hard to begin. But taking the third, fourth, and fifth step is much harder. The applause has faded. We have settled into new routines. The expectations have been set, communicated, and must be met. Momentum is now harder to maintain as new information, opportunities to fail, and expanded influences are presented on the other side of the open door.

The daily grind of routine and repetition of repeated tasks begins to taste like cold oatmeal devoid of flavor. Still packed with everything you need, but now it is monotonous, boring, and uninspiring. The journey beyond the first steps is also when failure hits harder. Falling short has a stronger impact on the mind, and showing weakness appears problematic. *I have gotten this far—I should know what to do.*

I have seen more leaders tap out not at the start of the race but midway through, after the promotion has happened and the first big bonus has been deposited. Within three to six months the grumblings begin like clockwork. The satisfaction and praise having now worn off. As the challenges mount, normal expectations become pressure points in the present.

Throughout our days, we go into situations in which we feel unprepared. The air becomes thinner the higher we climb, both personally and professionally, requiring us to adjust in new and unfamiliar ways as we struggle to find our breath in the thinning atmosphere, gasping as we attempt to adapt amid a potential loss of control. To regain some semblance of power, we decide to force God out of the driver's seat. How often have you decided to take the wheel from him, especially when you believe God is silent?

We need to be okay with dreams, visions, and prayers changing, just as we ourselves change. We must resist the urge to doubt our abilities and rethink our course of action each time we run into a new wall. Sometimes what seems like a broken dream actually holds components of what will be needed to propel forward.

CORNER FAITH

There are few greater joys than answered prayers or opportunities to walk in purpose. Having the ability to hold the very thing you have worked tirelessly toward is a reason to rejoice. You sacrificed and devoted a lot of time and energy toward this thing, person, or idea. You can look back and see exactly how God worked everything in your favor—where his hand was clearly on your life. He opened the door. He delivered on the promise.

When I was sitting in my car in the driveway, God had given me more than what I asked for: a booming career, access to wealth and professional networks, and healthy children. Yet the pressures and challenges on the other side of these doors often felt unmanageable.

My body was becoming sick. I brushed aside troubling signs, like frequent headaches, subtle indicators of a deeper unrest. The relentless stress of my career manifested in frequent migraines, their painful rhythm an unwanted reminder of responsibilities waiting. The hard-earned promotions would be the final straw atop an already crumbling marriage, while the demands of my career exacted a toll on motherhood that I was not prepared for. Soon, surrogate caregivers took my place as my absence stretched into long hours and endless travel.

There were many blessings in that season. Yet there was much more I needed to be prepared for, wisdom I needed to gain before taking the second, third, and fourth steps. But these were things I didn't even know how to pray for. When I look back, Romans 8:26 takes on a deeper meaning: "In the same way, the Spirit helps us in our weakness. We do not know what we ought to pray for, but the Spirit himself intercedes for us through wordless groans."

When things don't go according to plan in any area of life—in creative settings, projects you manage, parenting, personal medical situations—we find ourselves asking, "Did I get something wrong? How do I pray now? What happened to my life?"

But remember, just because something is new or difficult doesn't mean it's wrong. It doesn't automatically warrant a change of course. It also doesn't mean Jesus is no longer willing to carry your burdens or listen to wordless groans. This tension, the struggle of not knowing whether to change course or persevere through the moment, is something we will run into from time to time and should openly discuss in safe spaces. It's in these moments of uncertainty that we must recognize that we're not alone, even as every single thing appears to be falling apart.

What we sometimes fail to realize is that our stretching and growing does not stop once the steps forward have started or the prayers have been answered. God's care for us does not cease. We won't reach completion in this life. Pruning never ceases. Dead things must fall off to ready us for whatever is next, for future growth.

Attaining our dreams does not mean life stops happening around us. Nothing in the Bible or human history says that once someone has received the things they prayed, worked, and strived for, their aches suddenly go away.

Dreams do not always stay featherlight. Marriage takes effort. Careers require sacrifice. Friendships evolve. And raising children is the ultimate labor of love, requiring a nurturing that often pushes a parent to the brink. But in all this, God does not change, nor do his promises. The commitments he makes to us remain firm.

Isaiah 40:28 says plainly,

> The LORD is the everlasting God,
> the Creator of the ends of the earth.

He will not grow tired or weary,
     and his understanding no one can fathom.

Our relief sits in the tension of living in the "now and not yet." Not fully knowing what tomorrow holds but trusting the patterns of the One who holds tomorrow. Pushing beyond the personal failures of the moment, new sacrifices, present loneliness, or unmet expectations. Trusting not only that God will help us course-correct when needed but also that he is never surprised. He can see around every corner, and he never loses faith in his plan.

CAPACITY

In my driveway, with my hands tightly gripping the wheel, I could only focus on the "right now." I kept looking back at what I had hoped for and comparing it to what was. The disappointment of my reality washed over me. I had made so many promises to myself: I would be different, lead differently, think and move differently, be wiser than my years, and bounce back quicker. I promised to remain unrattled and unwavering no matter what, but I wasn't delivering on these naive promises to myself.

Here's the thing I've come to realize amid struggle: While we wrestle with failure or regret, God is gently helping us build the capacity to handle what is to come. He is not a bystander, but active, helping us to create capacity to face whatever lies ahead while also shielding us in the present. He prunes away what is not beneficial and lays groundwork through the vehicle of his Word, our failures, and our relationships. He not only prunes away dead branches but also cultivates the soil of our hearts. Meanwhile, as we mature, we learn from our failures and keep investing in meaningful relationships that foster growth. And so, the cycle continues. In these moments of struggle, he is teaching us invaluable lessons of resilience, faith, and the enduring power of his love.

It is possible that the things causing you to clench your fists around the car steering wheel will be used to prepare you for something greater than your right now. Just as it did for me. This means you may have to change your focus or adjust the commitments you made to yourself and others.

I believe we are made up of the promises that we have the boldness to make and keep but also the ones we know must be broken or changed altogether. As we gain wisdom, clarity, and access, our understanding of what we can handle deepens. We adapt and grow. None of this necessarily means we misinterpreted God's guidance or made poor choices. Rather, it signifies a shift in perspective—a realization that failure doesn't define our future happiness or success in new chapters.

You will find your ram in the thicket—the answers you seek from God. But sustainable growth and fulfillment do not reside in the convenience or the comfort of old chapters. They emerge from the courageous and resolute steps of personal faith.

While you may feel overwhelmed with your current circumstances, remember that seasons are not permanent. Embrace the opportunity to adjust and, if necessary, apologize. Your self-imposed promises, though significant, are not set in stone. You possess the power to change. So, set pride aside, seek peace, and thrive.

Stretching signifies a willingness for greater understanding, lessons, growth, and expectation, along with a dose of patience. It empowers your future endeavors, infusing them with purpose and determination, putting power behind your future pivots. Look forward and take your next steps boldly, for no one can do this for you. So loosen your jaw, breathe deeply, lean on God, and unclench your fists.

FOUR

GRIT

THE ART OF PERSEVERANCE

Throughout my younger years, I played basketball. Though I rarely touch the leather ball these days, I still remember the chill of the gymnasium as the lights flickered on for the first Saturday of preseason conditioning, a period of at least two weeks when athletes reacclimate their minds and bodies with sprints, a healthier diet, drills, and rest, preparing physically and mentally for the upcoming season.

I dreaded this opening part of the season. It pained me to think about what was coming.

Our lungs would burn as the coach's whistle blew, signaling that it was time to run another lap, complete yet another jump, do one more set of push-ups. As we stretched our limbs, the chill in the air was replaced with exasperated groans and the squeaks of new basketball shoes sliding across the floor. This steady cadence of rubber soles across waxed wood floors filled the space, the sound bouncing between the smoothness of the court and the dry soles of our shoes.

With each deep stinging breath, we clutched our sides, attempting to patch the pain and pace our breathing before the next whistle blew. The piercing sensation coursing through our limbs only affirmed what the coaches would yell over our huffing and puffing: "No one here is ready for prime time—back on the line."

Back to the line we would go. Back to suffering until our muscles, lungs, and minds were strong enough to endure beyond the drill.

Year after year, my teammates and I were reminded by our bodies that we were not in game-ready condition. Our coaches provided routine drills showing us how emotionally unready we were. The shame rarely stayed for long because being honest led to progress. Acknowledging where we were falling short in the present showed we cared about the outcomes in the future.

These first few weeks of the season were dreadful but necessary. I did not realize then how these lessons from my teen years would become valuable pillars well into my thirties and forties. When feeling the need to rush God's process instead of doing "the work" of readying, I remember what it felt like to walk into the gym during preseason conditioning.

PREPARATION

In the trenches of preparation, where the ground beneath our feet feels unstable, we confront adversity and uncertainty head-on. It is here, amid the waves of chaos, that the value of past lessons becomes apparent in our attempt to face forward and not look back. While hindsight may not always offer perfect clarity, reflecting on our experiences briefly provides perspective that guides us back on course after setbacks or moments of hesitation.

The benefits found in the stretching, twisting, and building we experience are bound together by diligence and preparation. What once felt like insurmountable challenges, unbearable aches we believed would certainly break us, now become stepping stones to progress.

The mention of preparation can cause some of us to wince or stiffen, as the thought of delaying desired outcomes or moving away from current comforts can be daunting. However, it is critical to recognize that preparation not only helps us bounce back from present challenges but also sets us up to navigate them more effectively in the first place.

Listen, I get it. We naturally want to sprint toward our version of victory, completion, or absolute answers. Whether because of fatigue, anticipation, or simply a lack of patience, at some point, we've all probably wished to avoid confronting areas of potential failure or inexperience. Throughout my two decades as an HR leader and executive, I've had unparalleled access to people's careers and witnessed many individuals bail, tap out, quit, or refuse to maintain focus before the clock even starts. Simply due to a lack of fight or the ability to bounce back or hold the line.

Listen up, when it comes to preparation, we are talking about grit and tenacity here. If anyone tries to tell you that the process of preparation is a cakewalk, they couldn't be more wrong. The topic of preparation tends to be skimmed over. Instead of emphasizing its power and the confidence it brings, podcasters, consultants, some church leaders, and mentors jump to living out your purpose. They expect tangible outcomes before asking us the really significant questions. I am not telling you not to dream, plan, or start again. Do it all. But before or after those first steps, let me ask this:

Are you ready?

How have you prepared?

And perhaps most importantly, how have you mended the wounds of the past?

These questions might stir up some discomfort. They require introspection, honesty, and a reevaluation of where you are presently. But facing them head-on, while looking forward, is critical for building resilience and navigating challenges with grace when life throws punches in your direction.

You will not win every battle you face. I am sorry, even with practice, surrounded by perfect teams and strong friendships, you will not always see victory. Remember, perfection, even the illusion of it, is owed to no one. Failure is a guarantee, and the trenches are where we learn how to properly place our expectations. Not only for others but for ourselves. I want you to fall in love with preparation, while not being bound by it. Preparation is not just about winning every battle; it's about building resilience and sharpening your skills. Just like with my basketball preseason practices all those years ago, it ensures you'll be stronger and mentally ready when the time comes to step into battle. So embrace the waiting. Enjoy the process of engaging with God about the big stuff without assuming it means you are stagnant. It is actually the opposite. Preparation is about focus and being in authority over your life. Preparation is about deciding to move with precision.

ACTION

No one desires to go backward. If we do, it's often because we fool ourselves into believing we would make different choices if we encountered the same circumstances again. But life doesn't provide a rewind button, so stop searching for one.

However, conditioning and planning reveal how we can prepare for the long haul, including the races we never planned to run. Whether we call it training, therapy, personal development, or peer accountability, what matters is understanding its significance to achieving lasting success.

These necessary stopgaps, temporary practices to help us improve in the long term, give glimpses of how we may handle parts of the road ahead. The challenges we face wait to pounce, drawn to some of us like a bee to pollen in the spring. While conditioning, we also see flashes of what is possible. We learn to watch for situations where we may misstep; need a guide, mentor, or leader; or will require more determination. *These winks of possibility in the waiting are what keep us going.*

No one wants to focus too long on the areas they see as "weakness." But at some point, you must stop pretending. To move forward, you must lean into the areas requiring attention; smiling and nodding will only get you so far. You will have to put in the effort of conditioning so you can show up and deliver.

You can't lead in your own life if you don't have an opinion on the direction you're headed. You can't punt decisions forever or bypass everything that makes you feel uncomfortable. If you do, here is the guarantee: You will remain stuck. You will likely remain dissatisfied. You will only grow so far. You will be lost in the fog of it all.

Certain lessons can be learned only under pressure and in action, not on the coattails of previous wins, other people's opinions, or external affirmations. You have to put things learned into practice, no longer allowing the fear of failure or rejection to keep you stuck in the mud.

As you put things into practice, watch out for regret and discouragement. When they make their presence known, they can become a threat to forward progress. Discouragement creeps in and we lose a little heart because we aren't ready *now*. The pressure begins to amplify our weaknesses and not our strengths. It becomes easier to remember when the lull or downtime wasn't taken advantage of.

Shut this thought process down now, and don't look backward. You have already made those choices, and who is to say they were the wrong ones? This is not time to shift gears in the direction of regret. You have experienced peace, victory, and joy before, and you will hold it again. Move forward and stop allowing regret to push you around.

If right now you are in a moment of duress personally or professionally, I want you to pause and sit with this. Sound decision-makers listen, ask questions, and *then* formulate an opinion or refine the ones they have. Which means you don't need to have every answer. You can leverage what you know and change as you grow without the fear of being wrong.

The ability to stay laser focused on the now, where your feet are currently standing, without a cloud of shame or regret, will help you shake off the desire to bypass what is needed for the future. This will also help you avoid the allure of looking in the rearview mirror even when progress does not feel immediate. When faced with closed doors and impatience is at your heels, don't abandon your preparation. As others appear to be outpacing you, continue to practice.

Continue to deepen your knowledge and, more importantly, your relationship with Jesus. Go to therapy, expand your community, or focus on your health. You may even need to move in silence as you widen your purview. During this time, gaps and shortcomings may bubble to the surface. Count that as a win, a priceless blessing. You now better understand your personal blind spots, the places where your vision is poorest. Equipped with this deeper insight, you're not only able to plan more effectively but also to articulate precisely the support or mentorship you require, without relying on assumptions. You can pray about these shortcomings in detail and gain wisdom before putting the lessons into practice.

Though your situation may seem heavy, keep moving forward. Once you find your rhythm in refining, it will become easier. Bouncing back will become second nature. You will no longer be easily knocked off course, because your eyes are locked and focused. Stay right in line with God and your abilities until you feel ready to sprint forward. Preparation and practice help us understand what sacrifices may be required and to calculate what we are willing to put on the line.

Here is a critical point I learned while advising leaders and individuals navigating complex situations: It is important to prepare, practice, and grow alongside those we feel safe with and who love and support us, the people who allow us to process from a distance but also close the gap when silence lingers for too long. During times of readying, we need spouses, partners, friends, family, and mentors to remind us of our trajectory and who we were before the stumble. They bring to light our strengths and past victories that may have slipped our minds while in the trenches. They point us forward as we strive for improvement and turn toward the future with resilience and grit.

Regardless of our personal achievements, we all need people who aren't afraid to say God's name and remind us of who he says we are, whether we're sprinting or crawling. If you don't have a person like this in your life, I'm here to step into that role right now.

You are capable. You are more than whatever obstacle, blunder, or relationship is holding you back. With the remaining breath in those lungs, move forward and prepare with purpose. No more excuses.

And where my words fall short, remember, God does not need rest, clarity, or a second wind. Where we are weak, he is strong (2 Corinthians 12:9). Yes, moving into action and preparation are messy, requiring a lot of personal honesty. But don't hide from it, because the sacrifices required will be well worth it in the end.

EDIT YOUR WAY TO BETTER

When I officially became a single parent back in 2017, my entire world shifted. Suddenly the phrase "bad parent" entered my vocabulary as I thought about how my life had detoured and the impact this may have on my young children. All my perceived "faults" and shortcomings were amplified. Missing school events, needing to depend on community more, and spending chilly evenings alone after the children drifted off to sleep reminded me of the simplest failures.

Fear and external deposits of shame told me these feelings were real and permanent, practically unfixable. Failures I could clearly see only intensified the war in my mind. I felt trapped, as if I were suffocating under the weight of expectations and judgments, both from myself and others. It seemed there was no escape from the relentless cycle of doubt and self-criticism.

To pull myself out of this spin, in the direction of better, even when my mind felt full of darkness, I asked myself a form of those critical questions mentioned above: How do I get ready for this part of my life? How can I better prepare myself for the future? And have I truly begun mending wounds from the past? Very little had been done on my part to address these challenges, but often progress starts in these moments of reflection following loss or self-doubt, when we recognize the need for change.

I had the power to change my perspective and take control of my narrative once I gave my strengths and victories, no matter how small they seemed, room to breathe. Deep down, I knew I was a phenomenal mother, providing for my children and regularly bringing joy to their faces. But this was all buried by wrong thinking and untruths. Slowly, and I mean slowly, because progress isn't usually lightning-fast, I discovered a newfound sense of resilience and determination. As I learned to trust my instincts, facing forward meant moving toward newfound grace and confidence.

Fear tells you that the ripple effects of failure are permanent.

Impatience whispers that time, not God, is in control.

Weakness attempts to place self-doubt in the driver's seat.

Put fear, impatience, and misguided views of weakness in their proper place. Here is the reality: no matter how deep and complex of a hole we find ourselves in, there is a way out. Mistakes and missteps may have different levels of consequence, but they aren't permanent. God is always in control, and his reach is infinite. He is never late, nor rushed by man's ticking clock. Always follow his still voice over the naysayers' logic and he will point you back to solid ground every time.

When we listen, God's voice tells us that those personal areas of weakness are only a portion of who we are. He wants to draw even closer to us, filling these gaps because in the places where we are weak, he is strong.

In some seasons our shortcomings seem almost deafening. During other periods they appear nonexistent. Never believe the roller coaster of emotions we all experience. You are never so far gone that your only options are to pretend, bypass, or tap out. No one is ever too far gone. I don't care what the shortsighted say.

I get it, you are fatigued, depressed, disheartened, or sick of all the performing. No judgment—I have been there. The very thought of embracing preparation, no matter how great the analogy used to motivate, can sound like delayed relief. More work, more effort, with no guarantee of a substantial return. You need an answer now! But stuck is not your final answer, nor is the stagnation you are draped around.

You must start somewhere. And right now, pretending, rushing toward a finish, making excuses, believing the lies you are telling yourself, and hoping good intentions will one day rescue you are not answers. Looking backward is not a route to the promised land.

Start by embracing this truth: *I can edit my way to better.*

Read that again. You can edit your way to better. You can hit the pause button and then start again. You can reapply the lessons in new ways, reroute the path based on new information, or pivot slightly. You can take time to pray. This is not just about changing your mind but taking leaps of faith with God. The key here is doing the journey with God, not going rogue. You aren't a bystander in your story, and neither is God; there is no need to simply react.

Considering all you have been through, you have earned the right to edit your way to feelings of relief and fulfillment. You can edit your way to freedom. With God you can rework your present with an eye on your future.

There's no need to remain tethered to past mistakes, weaknesses, or fears. We are going to break free by asking the right questions and listening closely enough to discern when we are receiving the wrong answers. Together, we're embracing tough situations, acknowledging the role heartache has played, and facing difficult people head-on. Life doesn't come with a giant eraser or a fast-forward button—there is no going back.

At no point should anyone disrespect your journey by saying "just move on." Simply moving on does not make you ready for prime time. Little growth is found in routinely avoiding stuff that makes us feel uneasy. Your leap, your courage, your strong footing will be found by accepting that you could fail. Be prepared to apologize and acknowledge the emotions lying dormant within you. Throw your shoulders into pursuing the life you desire, and remember to embrace God with open arms, leaning into his wisdom and strength.

Listen, you may need to change your expectations.

Some of this will be messy, sweaty, exhausting, and sometimes mentally weighty as you make tough decisions. But it also means you aren't stagnant; you are actively working toward your version of better. And if you don't get it right, go back to the starting line and do it again until the preparation becomes a part of your regular movements.

Here are three questions I ask myself as I face new challenges, experience disappointment, endure stretches of exasperation, and confront personal shortcomings:

1. Is this behavior change/dream/want doable?
2. Will I need other people? If so, when?
3. Is my ego leading this decision? Or is it based on reality?

These three questions are intended to help you gain focus and diminish your desire to rush through the tough parts of the journey. Answering these questions can help you develop perseverance. The answers aren't about saving face, gaining participation points, or racing against the "something to prove" ticking clock. It's about quieting the storm—the one inside you. It's about seeing the facts as they are and then building a plan based on your answers.

If you decide something can be done, it can in fact be done.

No one else can say yes on your behalf. Yep, we are back to you deciding what is important. Because even if those closest to you cheered endlessly, none of it matters if you don't have a yes for yourself. If no one has told you, in time, cheers can turn from something of substance into weightless vapors. So do this for yourself.

Whether it's financial planning, parenting choices, mental health decisions, starting a business, or quitting addictive behaviors, the decision-maker in your life is you. There is no way around this fact. Yes, even when the balance of power does not always appear to be in your favor. Even if you are too tired to try again right now, I need you to grab belief in yourself until you have enough fuel to get back up.

You believing something in *your* life is doable matters.

You understanding the type of people *you* need and when matters.

You acknowledging when ego (self-importance) versus facts are leading your decisions matters.

Partners, colleagues, teammates, friends, and family may have significant input, but when it comes to personal behavior changes, properly preparing, and refining your purpose, the buck stops with you.

Here is a reality check we all need: No one can run on the fumes of someone else's belief. But the power of Jesus can fully sustain us, even amid disappointment and stretching. No one can go through the trenches of preparation on your behalf; this part of the journey can't be punted. But walking in the peaks and valleys in lockstep with God can uphold us.

Though it is hard, here is the beauty of editing your way to better: it is the continual opportunity to assess what is needed, when you will need it, who is needed, and the whys behind the need. These four issues are linked. Don't stop at "what's your why"; also fully understand the need connected to it. This is how we see clearer.

For instance, if your "why" is to pursue a higher-paying job, the need behind that why might be the desire for financial stability or to provide a better quality of life for yourself or family. Understanding the need behind the why involves recognizing the motivations driving the desire, whether it's to alleviate financial stress, achieve certain goals, or pursue professional growth. Whatever it is, when we understand the need connected to our why, we make more informed decisions.

Within all these discoveries, folded throughout personal stretching, twisting, asking, and reshaping, we recognize our limitations. As we keep moving forward, even returning back to the starting line after failure, we find new ways to "get it right." We experience growth that comes with breaking our own rules. We learn what it means to embrace failure.

The more you edit your way to better, the more comfortable you will be with the process. For it is in the preparation that we see exactly where our capacity ends and where God continues and ascends. When fear, impatience, and misguided views encapsulate you during periods of exhaustion, foggy thinking, and emotional weariness, cling to God, ask yourself the three questions, and begin to edit your way to better.

STEADY

Preparation of any kind requires patience. Everything we have covered will require not only focus and humility but also patience. I would be shortchanging this conversation if I did not touch on how important it is to stay steady. The ability to hold yourself in place even as impatience enters the conversation will give you clarity and the strength to take bursts forward when needed. Sometimes your patience will be stretched as seasons of preparation extend longer than a few days or months. Hold firm and focus.

No matter how you cut it, preparation and patience go hand in hand. This includes patience with yourself, others, and the process. One without the other will skew your feelings and leave you unfocused.

Choosing "ready, set, go" over "ready, set, wait" causes greater potential for small missteps. As we hurry, we risk overlooking key insights or comments from others that could better inform decisions or improve our understanding of the situation. We walk into scenarios we could have avoided, if only we had taken a moment to slow down. Bypassing steps to save time or emotional processing adds more stress, causes clustered thinking, and introduces components of self-doubt on the back end of the journey. There is not a badge or more rewards for limping over the finish line. Rushing is not a requirement for success.

Here is the permission slip to embrace the life you want and not live so much of life on an empty tank. Preparation and the rigor attached to it will help you glide across the finish line. If you remember nothing else, take this with you: you can't bypass preparation, so allow patience to be your secret weapon.

Those things you fail to learn while in a rush will find you under pressure. So let the lessons "cook." Give yourself space to grow and to quiet the noise. Be self-aware enough to say, "I am not ready for [*insert your whatever here*] yet." None of this—preparation or patience—is about ensuring you "win" but understanding your needs. Leverage your community; they can be the ultimate defense and armor against mental hurdles, social pressures, personal gaps, and the challenges we face in the valley floor.

Wisdom is gained in battle. That's when everything we've learned can be tested under pressure. We also experience God in new ways every time we realize we can't do it all. Preparation is not about you becoming the expert, it is about gaining wisdom for future steps.

It takes grit to look at yourself and acknowledge what really needs to be done. The power of patience helps you not to bypass the progress found in the process. Pretending to be ready based on someone else's experiences is a copy-and-paste attempt that never lasts.

With humility, embrace the art of preparation and the conditioning of life, and you will persevere.

FIVE

RIPPLES

PROMISE KEEPER

What is that ringing sound?

I cautiously shifted my body and opened my eyes. I attempted to slow my breathing and absorb the unfamiliar noise. All I felt was the stillness in the room. I was irritated. I wanted to move. I needed to identify the sound. It seemed mechanical. I closed my eyes again.

Bingo! A mosquito zapper before it zaps. That's what it is. Oh, it's such an annoying noise.

I rolled over—and that's when I realized I wasn't sitting on a patio in Charleston, South Carolina, or on my deck in Ohio. It was 2:05 a.m., and I was lying in a hospital bed. And the ringing sound was from the bathroom light. A nurse had flipped it on. She was not apologetic about her presence, and I didn't find her humming of Ray Charles's song "Georgia on My Mind" amusing.

I sat upright. My body hurt from the tension it had been holding. Even the roots of my hair hurt. The room was spinning both fast and slow.

I blinked as a wave of nausea attempted to overtake me. I drew in a deep breath and pulled the blanket closer, staring at the IV in my arm. *Dear God, how did I get here?*

Just a few days earlier, I had been living according to a particular plan and detailed schedule. A few years prior, I had been promoted to a job that opened unimaginable doors for me across the globe.

In annoyance, I rolled my swollen, puffy, red-ringed eyes at the pressure and personal brokenness I felt as I lay in a cold hospital room. I was a few weeks away from turning thirty-seven. My head was spinning, making it clear that I couldn't focus on work. I found myself feeling restless and bored as I replayed my experience from the day before:

"Ms. Ricks, we believe you could be having a transient ischemic attack or TIA," a doctor had told me. I learned that a TIA causes people to temporarily experience stroke-like symptoms. It is the body's way of sending a warning signal. I was admitted immediately.

"How did I get here?" was all I could manage to think through the fog in my mind. It's the question that ran through my head as the doctor peppered me with questions and instructions. *How do you feel? Walk me through your day. What is your job? Smile hard. Are you married? Hold out your hands.* I fumbled my way through the responses as my brother calmly looked on. I saw his concern but ignored it because I had to be okay; I am *always* fine.

I sighed and thought again, "This cannot be happening. What will happen to my babies? Why has God left me? Is there nothing else left for me to do? Why is my body betraying me?" So many questions that no one could answer. But I also couldn't speak fully or think clearly. For the first time in my life, my mouth did not feel like moving at the speed I was accustomed to.

"Ms. Ricks, can you tell me your birthday?"
September 4.
"What year is it?"
Um, 2020.
"Who was the last person you spoke with?"
Silence. I had to close my eyes to think. Everything was so foggy.

"Ms. Ricks, who was the last person you spoke with?"

My brain was trying to push through the subtle ringing, the wave of questions, the fog, and the anger. My brain was misfiring and reaching for familiar responses. But with its attempt to shield and protect me, I was only becoming more concerned.

God, how did I get here? This wasn't a part of the plan, not even close. I was in the middle of a work crisis and living through a global pandemic. This was not a part of my plan, and it could not be a part of God's.

When our plans are disrupted, we assume God's plan is also. When we are discouraged, we assume God, too, has grown desperate or bored. But this is never the case. He is steady and forever focused on us and his glory. We are the ones who become forgetful, exhausted, and confused.

"Ms. Ricks, we are going to step out and let you change. A nurse will be in shortly to give you a COVID test."

Though my brain was fuzzy and my legs felt like jelly as I sat upright, I understood what the doctor had said. I was staying here because they were concerned.

I was officially tired of thinking and trying to

talk. I was so tired of responding, tired of fixing problems, and now my mouth was cotton-ball dry. I struggled to process everything happening. My body felt weird. My brain wasn't firing correctly; it was all delayed and distant. I felt hollow. I needed to feel something.

I smiled and blinked as everyone but one nurse exited the room. I followed her to the bathroom, aware that I was doing my best to appear normal. She turned on the light, and the brightness forced me to gain my bearings in a new way. She turned, smiled, and gave me clear instructions: Put on a very unfashionable hospital gown, place my clothing in the bag, and pee in the cup. I nodded. She exited.

The light was achingly bright, and the floor was bone-chilling cold. My teeth rattled from the combination of uncertainty, stress-induced muscle tics, and the strain of blurred vision. I slowly changed, my body stiff with fear and faked calmness. My soul clanked as I heard my brother talking to the staff on the other side of the door. I strained to make out the words, but my ears were tired. I was so tired.

I sat down on the toilet lid and took in a breath. *What am I supposed to be doing? I have forgotten something; I know it. What have I already forgotten? Why am I even in this bathroom?* I looked around slowly, attempting to shake my memory awake without making myself sicker. Finally, my eyes locked on a cup with dashes. Plastic cup. In my head, it sounded like "pl-as-tic c-up." *Yes, now I remember. Pee in the cup and give it to the nurse.*

When I exited the bathroom, I admitted I had forgotten one of the reasons I went in. The doctor nodded, wrote something quickly, and said they would run some tests to help us understand what was going on. As the nurse touched my shoulder, my worry attempted to rise, but I shoved it away and climbed into the bed.

A few hours later, after I had been thoroughly poked and prodded, the nurse left and I lay in the hospital room alone. I thought about my two babies. I curled my throbbing body into a tight ball. For the first time in a while, I acknowledged the value of having someone sitting with you in joy and sorrow and refusing to leave. My heart ached deeply as wounds I thought had healed attempted to reopen amid unanswered questions. *How did I get here?*

The nurse entered again and finished filling out the charts. She looked at me and said good night, then closed the heavy door behind her. The loud click of the door rang through my temples; even my toes hurt from the jolt of the vibration. Now officially alone, I shifted in the bed and asked God why. *How did I get here?*

I will never forget the soft words that ran through my spirit. They were direct, loving, and hopeful: "Rest. I go before you."

I shuddered. This wasn't the first time I had felt God tell me to rest, but for some reason, this time the words took root. In this room, the ability to receive these words felt different. He was not only telling me to rest but that he was handling my burdens, as he always had. He wants us to continually lean on him, never tiring of resting and depending on him.

I felt my spirit take a deep sigh of relief as I slid away from the driver's seat and relaxed my achy head on the chilly passenger-seat window. This was nice. With God by my side, not being in control felt right; even with tubes in my arm, I could breathe easier. I felt like a little girl climbing into her dad's lap and resting her head on his chest, counting the beats of his heart in her head: *lub-dub, lub-dub, lub-dub.*

My entire adult life had been a push and pull with Christ, a dance of drawing closer to him and then drifting away. But even if we push away from God or walk away, or wander away, through it all,

God both waits and chases. Remaining steadfast, he heals weary hearts, shelters us through storms, and never once turns his back on us. Not once.

I was so tired of looking over my shoulder. All I wanted was to be free. Not free from a person. Not from the business world. Not from artificial expectations. This time I wanted to be free from myself and all the plans. All the doing. All the changing and contorting for people. This couldn't be the end of my story, one with plot twists laced with suffering.

As the beeping of the machine measured both my heartbeat and breathing, I pulled the blankets close. My body soon succumbed to the weight of the day. Though my brain still hurt, I believed God's words to me: "I go before you." I didn't know what God meant or even his plans, but I trusted.

GOD IN THE TRENCHES

We don't need to wait for mountaintop moments to find God; he stands with us in the chaos, in the trenches, in the valleys. He walks alongside us as we walk on isolated dirt roads, as we sit in cobwebbed corners, and as we reflect on the memories of conquered or avoided mountains. He is present on both the well-trodden and the less-traveled paths, waiting for us in the in-between spaces.

Success does not always resemble the envisioned finish line. Sometimes, winning means finding the courage to reach toward hope in simple ways. We do this by finding solace and strength in the small everyday moments that remind us of God's presence and love. These simple acts, even when everything appears to be crumbling around us, offer profound reassurance and peace, propelling us forward, even when we may need to pivot or start over entirely.

Amid all the advice, what often gets lost is the wisdom that points us back to center, back to faith, back to the assurance that God is in the fight with us, not a mere bystander. Some trenches are unavoidable consequences of decisions made, but the comfort lies in the knowledge that God will never forsake us. Facing challenges head-on is difficult, but remember this:

Avoidance is your kryptonite.

Indecision is a costly decision.

Time is the greatest snitch.

These aren't just catchy phrases. The collision of these statements forced me to accelerate certain learnings, practice what was both within easy reach and challenging, and steadfastly fix my gaze on God, refusing ever to turn away again.

Avoidance can make us believe that turning away from a problem will make it disappear with time. But when avoidance becomes ingrained in our thinking, it can suffocate our desire to move forward or even work toward healing. We often dodge things we'd rather not face—conflict, health issues, heartache, financial troubles, embarrassment. In those situations, God's peace becomes the counterweight, a peace that transcends understanding. Facing what you've been avoiding allows you to hold courage in one hand and God's peace in the other. Confronting your struggles and burdens doesn't mean you're stagnant; it means you're ready to make decisions, run the play, or set a new vision.

Indecision is a decision, and a costly one. Each moment of indecision can fill your core with the regret of missed opportunities and the return of self-doubt. Embrace failure, make it part of your personal equation, and be firm on this: never let others force choices on you. Have the courage to make your own decisions.

Time, our relentless friend, tells the truth sooner or later. It brings light to the shadows, revealing our denials and humanity. Failures are meant to be learned from, not outrun. We see God not only in blessings but also in the gaps. With God, we can outpace what would have once destroyed us in a foot race.

Lying in a hospital bed, I realized I had conquered mountains but felt the weight of climbing without peace and clarity. God had shielded and guided me, but I wanted to do things my way. Refusing to step off the mental, emotional, and physical treadmill had led to a health crisis before my thirty-seventh birthday. The ripples had turned into a wave.

WHEN THE MESS CATCHES UP

I remain immensely grateful that God is not confined to mountaintops, the place it seems only great men and women stand and teach. He is present in the mess that we make and that this broken world creates. In the hospital, the consequences of my choices—my avoidance and indecision and the ticking clock of time—caught up with me. What will it look like when the mess catches up with you?

This question isn't intended to instill fear. Rather, to reclaim control means acknowledging that you might not have all the answers right now but that you know where you will lean amid the chaos. Allow me to say this:

We cannot jeopardize our mental health and expect continual victories.

We cannot neglect our physical health without consequences.

We cannot sidestep a relationship with Jesus and expect to feel whole.

We cannot take shortcuts and expect endurance on the long road.

God is the ultimate counterweight to our troubles. His whispers and Word are designed to help us pro-actively react when we feel paralyzed. He has the power to reroute what threatens to overtake us; he's committed to being our refuge. Psalm 23:4 (NLT) resonates: "Even when I walk through the darkest valley, I will not be afraid, for you are close beside me. Your rod and your staff protect and comfort me." The shepherd is vigilant in protecting his flock.

I found myself in the hospital because of years of choices, not because of God. Yet what was meant to break me only provided more strength and grit because, by then, I knew exactly where to lean. God will continually pave pathways toward victory in your life. Keep taking those steps forward; it's the third and fourth steps that weigh us down most. Discipline is the tool to propel us toward victory.

When I was on the brink of a stroke, my mind

raced. I grasped for hope, just as I had in moments of reflection during lonely flights, chaotic meetings, court hearings, and long car rides. In every instance, hope was present. God was there throughout. His assurance, "I go before you," empowered me to make decisions unforeseen around the corner and granted me the strength to cease striving and rest.

We must actively participate in our personal growth with God. When we're no longer victims to the waves crashing around us, we won't bend toward laziness, dissatisfaction, or a disengaged life, even in the face of loss or disappointment. Our hope, grit, and freedom are found in acknowledging his presence amid storms, trenches, or valleys. Or even in unfulfillment we feel after climbing mountains you thought would bring happiness.

No more avoidance. No more indecisiveness. Create space to think, and then take action. When the lies of yesterday hunt you down in the form of regret and loneliness, when thoughts attempt to put your mind in disarray, and when you realize you're following the wrong leaders, mentors, or friends, snatch the reins back. Lean directly on God as you cross over troubled waters.

SIX

EYES WIDE OPEN

THE DEATH OF COMPROMISE

You've done the work. You've prioritized and optimized every part of your schedule. You are reading devotionals and self-enhancement books, drinking more water, and evaluating your boundaries. Yet here you find yourself once again with nothing left in the tank.

Imagine this: Your tank, the very thing needed to propel you forward, is down to mere fumes. Life continues to happen all around you while simultaneously breaking you down. One minute God feels close. Then, like the images in a sideview mirror, he appears distant. Maybe even distorted. You are confused and have little space to rest, no room for the mind to stretch or allow careless words to fall wherever they please without causing damage.

To march forward or show some semblance of progress, you do what you've always done: you slip back into old patterns. You revert to rhythms and sound bites that are painful but bring the ease of familiarity. You take the comfortable steps that once served you but have since ceased to be beneficial. It's like wearing shoes that used to fit perfectly but now pinch with every step. Soon, within this old predictability, you find yourself being pushed close to an edge—so close, your toes ache from the task of keeping yourself upright. You're holding the burden of your idealized expectations while grappling with the edges of present circumstances or another bad decision looming in the horizon.

Eventually, you inhale—every breath a reminder of life, even in the chaos. Then you exhale while opening your eyes wide in search of better answers. You wonder how you arrived in this place yet again. Whether you should simply stand still and allow the challenges to pile up in the corner of "never dealt with" or if you should try something brand-new . . . again.

How did you arrive here? Who were you following? Or was it your own footsteps leading you toward this cliff? After the dust settles, because trouble does not last always, which line will you return to? Can you muster the courage to walk away from the problematic cliffs you're facing?

ACKNOWLEDGING THE SHADOWS

Living on this side of heaven means we must repeatedly deal with difficulties in waves, working in overdrive to keep our eyes focused on the mounting hurdles in front of us. The shadows dancing around the walls of your mind can become so real that they appear to be monsters that cannot be defeated. Fear of failure, judgment, vulnerability, change, rejection—all of them become real-life boogeymen. To diminish the power of these shadows, it's crucial to acknowledge them openly to ourselves and in some cases others.

When we convince ourselves that asking God for relief is too much or downplay the significance of Jesus's existence and impact, we engage in a perilous game. We think that if we keep our heads down, eyes covered, or blindly follow the loudest leader, the shadows will fade. Experience teaches us that this is far from the truth. In fact, as we approach moments of potential collapse, the temptation to justify stagnation or withdraw from the race altogether becomes stronger.

I have said it before and will say it again: you are meant to complete every race standing upright, not limping. Challenges will not simply vanish, some questions will remain unanswered, and shortcuts are a rare commodity. And if you haven't noticed, life tends to get tougher when we avert our gaze from God, fragmenting our hope into the unstable promises we discussed earlier in the book.

The edges you feel pushed toward aren't designed to be lethal but rather to tether you to fear, chaining you to past mistakes and trauma. You might feel lost, so far removed from any semblance of stability that returning to a sense of "safety" feels unattainable. Standing at the precipice of your cliff, you may find yourself questioning, grappling, yet hesitating to act. But here's the truth: I believe you are capable of reordering your steps without missing a single beat and bringing God back into focus.

FINDING THE LINE

I often talk about ledges and cliffs, metaphors that reflect our decision-making processes and thought patterns. Life tests most of us on multiple fronts—faith, parenting, self-management, health crises, and more. Some say, "Under pressure we are perfected," but pressure isn't always about building perfection. There are times when life's pressures crack us wide open.

In these moments, unwanted thoughts, people, and behaviors can slip in, and we harden in different ways from the struggles thrown our way. We may choose seemingly easier routes, hoping to bypass certain trenches, clinging desperately to the fragile threads of progress, resisting yet another restart after losing sight of our goals, and praying not to become more weary or distant. We find ourselves living many parts of life on the edge.

One challenge we all face at some point is how to maintain our character under pressure. I've witnessed individuals pushed to their breaking points, standing at the ledge of "I thought I would never . . ." because they gave no care to whom they were following. They paid no attention to the direction they were being pulled, and they placed no personal limit on how far they were willing to go for money, power, or access. The conversation of how far is too far is seemingly universal.

I once worked alongside a brilliant woman, one

of the smartest businesswomen I've ever encountered. Over the years, seemingly insignificant compromises started rattling her moral compass and solid foundation. We often found ourselves sipping coffee, discussing business decisions, and pondering what God, family, and others thought about our lack of boldness.

She felt trapped by the life she had built, and appeasing people had become a part of the hamster wheel. Compromise by compromise, inch by inch toward the precipice, she was being tested at every angle. Behind closed doors, two successful women pondered what decisions they would want their children to make if they were in their seats. Naturally, they would encourage their children to push back, assert themselves, and stand firm.

However, she had already crossed her personal threshold of "too far." Her previous actions had set a precedent, leading her to believe that it was acceptable to do it again. But the lens of precedent is not always our friend. She had been silent before, so her perspective said she could do it again and still have a semblance of happiness. Her choices had reduced her capacity to resist.

Have you found yourself in this place? Twisted up by the knee-jerk reaction to please someone or chase something, convinced it will bring happiness or reprieve? Pushing yourself closer to the edge due to loneliness, financial insecurity, or the relentless ticking of the clock? Considering all this, the question you must ask is this: *Where is my line?*

Many desire to "get ahead," and it's fascinating to observe the sacrifices people are willing to make—sacrifices I, too, was once willing to make. Colleagues, mentees, online influencers, and others have morphed right before my eyes. Many have gone too far, influenced in character-altering ways. Suddenly, what was important to resist before becomes "Well, just this once." Some decisions lead to significant moral lapses, financial ruin, job loss, crumbling marriages, or even mental breakdowns.

My personal compromises around "I will never . . ." have pushed me to many breaking points because everything has a cost. Conforming to appease others has no limits or regard for your well-being. Conforming is coming for your backbone and, more importantly, your character. When these two are placed on the ropes, endurance is in short supply. Right now, whatever edge you are standing on, searching for answers, I want you to open your eyes.

You can't make sound decisions about next steps with your eyes closed. I can't tell you the right choice or what step to take in this moment, but I do know when compromising your character is on the line, pause. Then do the opposite. Yes, this is easier said than done, but your compromises are not free. This is about you deciding, once again, what you stand for, even if you have gotten it wrong in the past.

The sustaining power behind your "no" will be fueled by unwavering character. If you're unsure what traits you want to embody because you've been in the fog too long, study the life of Jesus. His leadership and relentless commitment to truth, empathy, and consistency are something we can all benefit from.

Before you find yourself in another complex situation, before you compromise *too* far, before getting in line behind another leader who will force you to conform and move away from your center— determine where you will draw the line. Failing is not a variable here. You can bounce back from most situations with time and patience. But compromise and indecision can easily push us over the edge.

GUIDING PRINCIPLES

Now let's talk about some solutions. This is not just about you walking away from the edges keeping you bound and the quicksand pulling you under. This is also about opening your eyes to the decisions you are making and the constant loop you stay in, those repeated rhythms no longer benefiting you.

See, this is the main problem with circles, the loops I am referring to: they keep us stuck. The allure is, there are no sharp turns, no major warning signs. Circles are predictable and familiar. But the danger is in moving but never progressing or changing.

I want to share three principles meant to help you see clearly and break away from behaviors that aren't beneficial: elevating, positioning, and influencing. These practices emerged from moments of failure but ultimately served as lifelines, pulling me out of a rut and shaking me free from old habits.

ELEVATION

"Rise above the fray."

Back in 2015, my mentor, Denise, spoke these words to me while in a coaching session about a decision involving many layers, opinions, and personalities. "You must decide to rise above the fray to make a clear decision," she said, leaning forward. This simple statement wasn't merely advice; it was a challenge to look beyond the noise of others vying to influence an outcome, the mental refusal to be overcome by the chaos in my mind or the office politics. I was compelled to make a silent declaration connected to character—who I was and what I stood for—a promise never to allow people or things to disrupt me into wayward submission. Denise's words to me were not only about decision-making but leadership. They spoke to self-regulation and courage even in the face of adversity.

Yet, simply saying you will rise above is not enough. You must set the terms of engagement. You must ensure that, no matter the exhaustion you feel or the obstacles you encounter, you are continually living out Romans 12:21: "Do not be overcome by evil, but overcome evil with good."

Take my experience with anger, for instance. I've learned to guard against situations that trigger it, recognizing that once these high emotions take the wheel, my decisions lose clarity, empathy dissipates, and my natural calmness goes out the window. Emotions shouldn't dictate outcomes, and opinions should never knock you off-balance.

Have your emotions ever determined the outcome before you had time to understand the facts? Are opinions knocking you off-balance? Endurance and mental fortitude demand discernment—knowing when to start, stop, and continue. Allowing others to influence your emotions prematurely can lead you over a cliff. Denise's counsel is a framework, not for arrogance but for the time needed to embrace thoughtfulness, feelings, and a solid response. It's a guide, including three fundamental starting points when you need to elevate your thinking:

1. Process the actual issue by saying clearly what the issue is.
2. Determine whether your perspective should change.
3. Hear God in *his* voice, not through the mouthpiece of others.

As you work through all of this, keep in mind that people will expect you to match their energy and urgency. Queue again, one of my favorite statements: You don't have to respond in the moment. There is no requirement to have an opinion on everything. And one of the key components of sound judgment is knowing when to be silent.

Elevating yourself above the noise of others' opinions and getting God's perspective allows you to take control of how and when you respond, not controlling others or how they feel. This is about no longer allowing people to pressure or influence you into decisions you aren't ready to make.

POSITION

While the term *evil* may evoke discomfort, it's an unfortunate reality that not all intentions are pure and corruption lurks both seen and unseen. Personally, I've faced emotional, spiritual, and monetary exploitation due to an unwillingness to acknowledge this darker side. I'm certain many share similar stories.

How often have you found yourself in the middle of chaos you had no hand in creating? You might feel so far down the road that it seems like stepping back could cause more harm than good. Disengaging may be significantly more detrimental than proceeding until the dust settles. If this feels even remotely familiar, consider these two questions:

1. What is the posture of my heart?
2. What is the real motivation behind my actions?

Answering honestly will help you properly position yourself, pointing your feet in the right direction without being caught in the loop of regret or the drive to prove others wrong. It forces us to do internal inventory while we are processing through what the best next step might be.

Strong character can't endure a compromised heart. The fight is lost each time. Allowing ourselves to be dragged into the pleasure of vengeance, corruption, dishonesty, or unhealthy vices puts us in a house of distorted mirrors, questioning how we went over the line and wondering, How did I get here? or Who have I become?

There have been times when I felt my heart harden in the midst of deep heartache or disappointment. A thick layer grew over the top of parts once butter-soft because I stopped paying attention to the real motivation behind certain decisions. I forgot Romans 12:19 (NKJV): "'Vengeance is Mine, I will repay,' says the Lord." Slowly my focus had shifted away from the important principles such as compassion, sound judgment, and respect for others.

There are many reasons our hearts become hard or our vision foggy: hurt, financial struggles, a broken heart, an affair, grief, disappointment, or coming face-to-face with our humanness. Whatever the reason, when our vision is compromised, we make compromises.

I've learned that justifying small compromises is not something that "just happens."

"Above all else, guard your heart, for everything you do flows from it," Proverbs 4:23 declares. In everything, we must work to soar above the things coming against us, while being anchored to the Truth. We are not to go through life as bystanders or fearful participants, but with our eyes wide open.

We should also pay close attention to the heart posture of the people we follow. Their words influence our decisions, and, naturally, with time we trust their guidance. The people closest to us can have a significant impact on our character and life. They can also knowingly or unknowingly lead us astray if they don't have a strong personal compass.

While we may not always choose our leaders, we certainly have a say in who influences us. Discernment is simpler than we think: fruit doesn't lie, and consistent behavior reveals true character. Grab the reins of your mind, heart, and spirit, and discern wisely. We are our patterns. Yes, people can change, but a pattern is a pattern.

Through God's grace, I figured out what was too far before crossing several lines, though not without some damage being done. You, too, can avoid compromise by setting boundaries, guarding your heart, and understanding the motivations behind your choices.

INFLUENCE

"Praise pays" but applause fades. In the realm of social media and during a time when seeking constant validation seems normal, it's easy for praise to become a driving force, making ordinary individuals want to be godlike figures. The pursuit of likes, money, and popularity often leads people to compromise their character, creating a fragile cornerstone that, over time, proves detrimental to the heart and mind.

The truth is, whatever can distract or overtake our thoughts will be the thing we return to repeatedly. Distractions are addictive like sugar, providing a temporary high but lacking the sustenance needed for genuine friendship, loyalty, or viable solutions. We crave the familiar when we are wading through predicaments, feeling lonely or unproductive, or becoming weary from the continual internal wrestling.

If you want to overcome some of the small obstacles pulling you toward the edge, here is a piece of advice as you rework your steps with God by your side: take time to understand the distraction, the why, and who is influencing your choices. Consider evaluating the long-term consequences of giving in to these distractions. Are the distractions worth compromising your values, goals, or character?

Walking away isn't always an immediate option. Sometimes the challenge lies in seeing the reality of your situation, not the hopeful illusion. Hope without fluff is what I want for you. Life throws us situations requiring endurance, especially when the answer seems just out of reach. We can become lost when we aren't paying attention to where we are going. Our heads are down because we are carrying a heavy load or just too tired to even think about the next step.

While this book won't solve every challenge you encounter, it does provide a critical insight: following the wrong advice and relinquishing control over your life make only exacerbates difficulties. Proximity to those who claim to have answers but lack substance is an empty promise. Proximity does not equal friendship, loyalty, or faithfulness.

Remember, you are in control of your journey. You decide what influences you, what won't overtake you, and what won't weigh you down. Consider this: Would you follow yourself? If duplicated, would you trust yourself with the decisions you're making? Evaluate the involvement of those you trust most. You possess the ability, with eyes wide open, to rise above the chaos, to evaluate your heart's posture under pressure, and to assess the influence that others are having on your character and decisions.

You have what it takes to pull yourself away from the ledges, one decision as a time.

SEVEN

NO FURTHER

LESSONS ON BOUNDARIES

When my children were very young, I purchased a beautiful house on a hill in Ohio. One of the reasons I purchased this house was because of the view. The main floor windows allow you to see the rolling hills and old trees; you can experience the change of each season, no matter the angle. In the mornings, I am often found sitting in one of the chesterfield chairs, with a view overlooking a pond.

On move-in day, my children sprinted across the cream-tiled floors weaving throughout the rooms. Zion and Londyn laughed, excitement in their eyes, touching every wall with their chubby fingers. Once they had their fill of climbing the stairs and exploring the hidden spaces, they shifted their attention to discovering what adventures awaited outside.

As my best friend and I walked through the tree-lined yard, shadowing the children, my son took off in a full sprint. The other children followed, giggling and screaming as children do when dancing in the sunlight. Like a wagon attached to a horse, my steps locked with his, quickening as he turned the corner and headed downhill with all the steam a young boy can muster— toward a beautiful body of water. Zion's legs moved fast through the grass, but in this instance, I was faster.

As parents, we spend our lives trying to outrun our children. We run far enough ahead to build bridges sturdy enough for them to sprint across. We help our kids grow wings strong enough to withstand the troubling winds that will surely blow. We stay steps ahead to create soft landings, anticipating when they may fall. We run, sprint, and jump as long as we can to keep them safe. We live out Proverbs 22:6, training them up in the way they should go, by laying some semblance of a path for them to follow. Until one day, they run right past us.

Halfway down the hill, I crossed in front of Zion, cutting off his adventure in one swift motion. Swooping him under my arm, I used the momentum to cup his body, resting his weight on my hip. His legs were still moving in wobbly circles. His belly shook with giggles, assuming we were playing a game. My chest pounded with fear of this new, very present danger.

Boundaries protect more than internal peace. In some cases, they serve as barricades against tangible threats, shielding us from harm. Panicked on the inside, I grappled with how to ensure the physical safety of my children while preserving their joy. How could I keep them safe and not exaggerate my own fear? The answer did not come immediately, but the water wasn't going anywhere, and neither were we.

A few days later, I walked both children down to the edge of the property. Bending over, I looked into my son's happy eyes, pointed to the rocks decorating the property line, and said, "Zion you can only go this far and no further."

This far and no further. Never did I think this simple phrase would change my relationship with boundaries and leading.

SETTING BOUNDARIES

In the ebb and flow of life, we often find ourselves drawing lines in the sand—markers that define respect, mental well-being, and self-care. These lines, however, aren't immune to the relentless waves of opinions, burdens, and complexity that can wash them away. My perspective on boundaries has undergone a transformation over the years, the lessons shifting like old gears in my mind as I navigate the evolving landscape of setting and respecting boundaries.

This topic is nuanced, with more than a few sharp edges. As we seek answers to enhance our lives and maintain our footing, self-reflection becomes crucial. When it comes to boundaries, the courage to set or respect them is gained not through projection but through self-reflection. So let's focus here on empowering you with a fresh perspective on this topic.

When I stated the phrase "this far and no further," nothing in me was ready to figure out how to personally set boundaries at home, in workspaces, or in broader communities. Yet God has an interesting way of meeting us in our mess.

After the conversation with my son, he persistently asked to go to the water, my response remained, "Not yet." I watched closely, reiterating the reasons why he wasn't ready. In the years that followed, both children learned to swim, becoming comfortable with water and understanding how to be safe. Without hesitation, they outpaced my deep fear. And I outgrew the fear of that pond, watching both my children step closer to the edge, testing the lines I had drawn. As they grew, their understanding, resolve, and tolerance increased. Eventually, I decided those old boundaries were no longer needed.

The point is that boundaries do keep us safe, sometimes in unseen ways, but they can also expire. If we aren't careful with the boundary conversation, we become trapped by the rhetoric, telling stories under the fearful cloak of "what if" or applying old scenarios to new people.

Not all boundaries are copy and paste. Some people and situations are different, and some formulas may no longer work and should change. Certain standards, though appropriate at the time, may no longer apply. New seasons may require an adjustment in boundaries, and you are empowered to change. Thrive outside the familiar comforts, and allow the lines to morph as experiences deepen your perspective and resolve. Fear and failure should not be the final decision makers.

My children have grown wiser and stronger over the years, stepping beyond the old lines, running closer and closer behind their mother's weathered heels. I want you to live a life so free that you can confidently declare "this far and no further," no matter the season. But I also want you to feel comfortable changing and deciding when old rhythms no longer serve you.

It would be wonderful to say this lesson with my son immediately helped me recognize my conflicts with boundaries, but life is not a movie. So I continued struggling with how to draw lines within my own life, even as I brought the phrase "this far and no further" into the workplace. Using words born from the fear of my children drowning, I now use them as a guiding principle to help others as they navigate complex conversations with their leaders and peers.

Though every surface quote should not become a foundation we build upon, "this far and no further" resonated with colleagues and friends. However, my professional hypocrisy regarding this topic was about to make its presence known.

OWN IT

Boundaries have become a popular topic, often discussed in terms of what the word signifies, how to set them, and how to respond to those who disrespect our wishes. Entire books have been dedicated to the subject, yet the focus tends to veer away from the boundary *crosser*, conveniently labeled as "toxic" or "narcissistic." These buzzwords provide an easy escape from self-inventory—after all, who wants to be stamped as toxic?

It's convenient to look at our actions while avoiding true self-reflection. We might get caught up in to-do lists or seek quick improvements, giving little time to pondering how our actions, words, and thoughts impact those around us, especially in the context of setting boundaries. In the spirit of being honest, I want to talk about this topic from a different and less savory vantage point.

After I brought the idea "this far and no further" into the workplace as it related to employees setting boundaries with leaders, God held up a large mirror. Suddenly I saw a giant plank in my eye, similar to the one referenced in Matthew 7:3–5. As I pointed out inconsistencies and lack of respect in leaders toward their teams, I was, unbeknownst to me, one of the difficult people needing navigation. God, in his gracious way, held up a mirror, exposing my glaring blind spot.

There are many reasons why I love God, but at the top of the list is his willingness to show me who I am without causing a scene or making me feel worthless. Like any good parent, God will correct us in private first. If we are paying attention, these nudges become opportunities to correct our behaviors.

In a business meeting, challenging a fellow leader's judgments about the team's commitment, I confidently outlined all the ways he (we will call him John) was wrong.

"John, you can't judge someone for this life change."

"A lack of availability does not mean the person lacks passion."

"John, who are you to judge the answer to a question you never asked?"

He listened as I gave recommendations on how to course-correct. But as I spoke, I clearly recall my stomach knotting as my words to him bounced back. It was like I was hearing them for the first time.

The echo slapped me to attention. And there is nothing quite like the smack of our own words when we suddenly realize *we* may be the problem. The mirror was up, and there stood my glaring gap. I felt queasy. What did I see that made my stomach churn? A pattern of silently assessing a person's ability to lead, desire to complete tasks, or emotional capacity, based on their willingness to move their boundaries for a corporation. Have you ever judged someone's "why" without context when they communicated a need, said no, or said not yet? If so, you understand what I saw looking back at me.

God, in all his sovereignty, would not allow me to lead from the front blindly. He tenderly provided this lesson to show me a personal flaw. God, in his wisdom, tilts our attention toward our words and experiences to illuminate the areas where we need improvement, gently nudging us to correct our behaviors. Seeing ourselves in someone else can be painful. Finding out we are the problem is disappointing. It takes grit to keep looking at ourselves after seeing parts we don't like.

Someone setting boundaries doesn't mean they have emotional, mental, or spiritual inabilities or shortcomings. We move into the realm of hypocrisy when we say we'll respect boundaries but turn around and refuse to accommodate someone's boundaries or judge or punish them because they held the line. If we find ourselves doing this, we must ask: Who am I to say this person's line is not important? Who am I to demand an explanation? Who am I to use "no" as a measuring stick for potential, loyalty, or love?

Over and over again, I had put my personal needs, wants, and desires above someone else's.

In my mind, "lack of flexibility" meant "not committed."

"Stretched too thin" meant "unable to handle stress."

"Unavailable" meant "lacking leadership."

"No" translated into "disrespect."

The evidence was clear. I was disregarding what others needed or communicated, especially when their boundary was inconvenient for me. None of this is easy to admit. My shoulders tense up just thinking about how easily I viewed my wants as better than those of others. But I believe there is always a chance to make things right, especially when God corrects us.

I want you to hold all the lines in your life that you feel are appropriate; own them. But have respect for others' boundaries as well, and take accountability for any missteps.

ACCOUNTABILITY

Our reaction to others' boundaries serves as a mirror to our own character. It's paramount to hold ourselves accountable for how we impact people's feelings, even when it pushes us outside our comfort zones. How we treat individuals, especially during vulnerable moments, speaks volumes. Effective leadership demands a willingness to embrace accountability for our actions and responses, recognizing the significance of upholding the values we profess.

No one should have to sift through endless books or social media feeds searching for ways to safeguard their mind just because someone struggles with self-regulation. As a community, it's crucial to call out those who dismiss others' thoughts and feelings. While I've learned much from personal experiences, my greatest lessons haven't come from building my own fence but from helping others build and reinforce theirs.

If we don't fully lean into this topic, failure, fear, and self-doubt will consume us via the vehicle of selfishness, with overwhelmed riding shotgun. Only by acknowledging and then addressing these inner struggles head-on can we hope to develop genuine empathy and support for others, free from the distractions of our own insecurities and fears. So before I could fully champion others, in the purest sense, I needed to deal with how I responded to what others needed, especially when I didn't have context. Some things are none of our business. Someone holding to their boundaries isn't a permission slip for us to judge them, make assumptions, or weaponize their "this far and no further" against them.

You're in charge of your life, not someone else's. You decide your needs and when to act on them, but you can't make these decisions for others. Judging others' boundaries reflects a lack of maturity and a reliance on personal comfort. I say this not in pride but in humility after learning from my own failure.

When someone crosses the line, choosing their wants over someone else's communicated needs, it's wrong. Failing to show up with empathy or provide space for freedom, even if in thought, not words, is also wrong. To do better, irrespective of the situation, the first step is acknowledging the need for behavioral change.

There have been several instances when I was the problem, and I make no excuses. This is the terrain of growth, the place where budding starts, and where lessons can blossom into something useful. Inner leadership—leading from a place of self-awareness, self-improvement, and self-management—is about routinely tackling the hard stuff. We must face the roughest parts of ourselves, look the grossest aspects of our behaviors in the eye, and deal with them head-on.

Yes, you may need to stop and start, but inner

leadership is about routinely tackling challenges. My concern is not about how you moved off your mark but getting you back on track.

Owning how we treat others, even if there no evidence of reckless behavior for people to point to, is a sign of growth. The cornerstone of impactful leadership, parenting, friendship, and loving your neighbor is recognizing that sometimes the problem is you, even when you're responsible for teaching the lesson.

There is no acronym here. No work-arounds. So I made professional adjustments, creating space for people to feel seen and heard.

Where I once condemned people's "lack of flexibility" I started to ask, "Can we find a better time?"

Where I once judged others who felt they were stretched too thin, I could now see that we needed more people on this project.

When someone said they were unavailable, that meant the person was unavailable.

We can't always be at everyone's beck and call. Their version of "no" allowed me to make an informed decision based on availability or bandwidth. No longer was I operating from a place of entitlement or offense but shifting toward clarity, understanding, and empathy.

If you've felt agitated when others don't respond as

you prefer and their boundaries seem incomprehensible, remember—it's not about you. The precious boundaries others set aren't about your convenience, and you're not entitled to know their origins. What's crucial is understanding your role in the conversation and not making others' boundaries about your comfort. Start holding yourself accountable today.

REAL SELF-CARE

Boundaries help ensure nothing pierces our peace. Now, let's delve into what "this far and no further" means from a different angle. A few years ago, I traveled to visit a friend who resides several states away. What was meant as a celebration became a situation that took months to fully process. During the visit, this friend decided to use such profoundly racially charged language that left me utterly speechless.

We have all been disrespected or found ourselves on the receiving end of hate. Words intended to shame can carry a sting that does not always fade with time. Throughout my career, I have been called a c**t, n*****, b****, and w**** to my face—in hallways, meetings, or while walking through campus.

Each time, the words were meant to evoke a reaction, tossed my way in a fit of anger by another person. The stories are countless. Having to navigate the appropriate response to hate, anger, and shame-filled words in workspaces, church, or at home can be a full-time job. As we all know.

However, this was a friend. My guard was fully down as the words landed. I had never dealt with a friend crossing the line in such a hostile way, tossing hate speech around with such ease. For the first time in a long time, I felt as though a person I loved put gasoline on a boundary—an uncrossable line—looked me in the eye, and lit the match.

We can discuss reinforcing our needs and wants within personal relationships for days. But when someone we love shatters us, the repair is rough, no matter what. Boundaries are a way of telling people how far they can go. These parameters also communicate how much you respect and value yourself. Even when the answer is not obvious or changing, these lines should never be crossed.

When boundaries are crossed so aggressively and intentionally, we must walk away without discussion. That's right: some behaviors should be met with confident silence. This is counter to what some gurus say, but this type of audacity should be matched with a declaration of internal peace. Here is your permission slip to disengage.

After I gathered myself and went through the motions for the remainder of the evening, I decided this person would never see or speak to me again. Did I wrestle with whether I should have a conversation with her? Sure. But with such violent language used, it felt like a gross violation of love and respect, and I remain comfortable with my choice. Also, sometimes we must hand people over to their god.

Some may label this as "ghosting," insisting on giving the violator a chance to apologize. Even in less dramatic situations, my advice remains the same: a conversation is not always owed to the other person. Consider this your permission slip.

You are not a hostage to disrespect.

You are the gatekeeper of your peace and God-given joy.

You are worth more than a reactive apology.

Silence is a powerful way of reinforcing stated boundaries.

This former friend knew what she did, and to manage the vile behavior, I cut the tie. You can do the same in your life. With actions and words, you declare, "This far and no further." I don't care who you are or what mistakes you've made. I've made plenty—you are reading about some of them. Yet none of this devalues who I am at my core. Mistakes shouldn't result in receiving less, being mistreated, or being reminded over and over again of where we went wrong.

If you are struggling with this concept of maintaining boundaries or walking away from certain relationships, I want to ask this:

Do you respect yourself?

Do you respect yourself enough to actively protect your peace, purpose, and healing?

Does something in you need to adjust? For example, have you been prioritizing the needs and feelings of others over your own?

Your lines, needs, and wants will shift depending on the season you are in and the growth you are ready for. There are times when you may feel as though fighting to maintain boundaries is not worth the effort. Maybe old boundaries are keeping you from moving forward, hindering the growth you are working toward. You might believe your failures mean you must give in to the needs of others, but this is not the case. You have every right to prioritize your well-being and set boundaries that align with your wants and needs no matter the season.

Real self-care is not soft. It takes time and is a

nuanced process. It involves recognizing that you deserve respect and honor until your last breath. "This far and no further" is about setting boundaries until they expire or need adjusting. Growth involves showing up as you are and deciding to change, a process that doesn't happen without strain, stretching, and embracing failure.

EIGHT

PRIORITIES

DECISIONS WITH EXECUTION

I was once participating in a Women's History Month panel when I was asked how to manage competing priorities. By this point in my career, agitation had officially set in as I watched people jump on the hamster wheel of corporate life, attempting to keep up with work demands and manage unrealistic business expectations, personal life needs, physical and mental health, and future dreams. The answer that came out of my mouth surprised me: "Start by knowing what to pick up."

A pause followed my statement, and the audience fell silent. Slowly, I observed figurative tiny light bulbs go off above the heads of the overworked and underappreciated—those always being told to juggle more glass balls and then figure out on the fly what's essential while walking and chewing gum.

A fellow panel member leaned forward and asked me to expand further. "Prioritization is about choosing each day, proactively, what is important. And then, from there, decide if an adjustment is needed. At times this will occur hour to hour or minute to minute. Give yourself permission to do this. We should pick up only what we can carry and, as leaders, be self-aware enough to know when the load is too much . . ."

Later, as I walked to my car, my feet were aching from the new high heels I was breaking in. I found myself wondering once again about prioritization and the discussion we'd just had. As an HR executive, I knew that prioritizing took more than someone boldly proclaiming that it's okay to put things down, pause, or proactively decide what is worth grabbing. Honestly, at that time, I hadn't even figured it out myself. I was surrounded by many people, meeting their demands as best I could, but the reality was that I, too, was drowning.

Climbing into my car, I removed those uncomfortable high heels. I softly rubbed my foot and leaned back on the hot black leather seat. As I closed the car door, the screen of my car flashed my assistants' names. At the same time, I had an instant desire for black coffee. This always happened when I knew stress was headed my way. As if on cue, a throbbing pain down the right side of my neck made itself known, letting me know a headache was riding shotgun. During this season of my life, I often wondered if I was truly placing my "wants" in front of my relationship with God. Or, in an effort to do more, be more, and hold more, was I making him a footnote in the story? I didn't have to think for long. The answer was yes. Yes, I was.

But on this day, like so many others, there was no time to process or do anything with this knowledge. After I had ignored my assistants' calls, my boss called with a crisis that would imprint the day in my memory. The coffee—and hopefully the migraine—would have to wait.

GETTING INTO ALIGNMENT

What does setting priorities have to do with making decisions, overcoming obstacles, and recentering yourself? The short answer: a lot. Many of us are stumbling through life trying to manage a career, our mental health, and our personal relationships—but in reality, many of us are drowning. Logically, we know we're not the only one trying to stay afloat, but we often feel like we're treading water alone. Trying to find ways to reclaim hope and move forward has come up throughout this book. But being able to find God in the chaos is a challenge, no matter how powerful the motivational quotes we read in passing. A key aspect of swiftly and confidently applying the themes discussed here hinges on discerning what is a true priority.

So where do we start when even the solutions are daunting and overwhelming? How do we find time to change? Will it be worth all the effort? Persevering can feel impossible, no matter how much grit you have. It's like moving in quicksand: slow, laborious, and difficult. Advice like "work smarter, not harder" sounds great during motivational speeches and short clips. But it can be extremely difficult to put into practice, let alone sustain. How do we find a sustainable rhythm when we live in an unpredictable world, and when every part of our life is screaming at us that it is a priority?

BLURRED VISION

When I think back, there was a time when I often felt at the end of my rope. During this period, I would attempt to engage God for a quick fix. There never seemed to be enough time to "be still." Someone was always calling. A child was always crying. Or some kind of chaos needed to be addressed. It was the pressure, not a desire to meet God and grow the relationship with him, that was making me to turn my gaze toward heaven. Despair forced my knees to bend in a posture of humility. But similar to what some feel after attending Sunday service, shortly after, I would find myself once again consumed by "stuff."

Over time, this rhythm of despair can become normal. We sometimes even justify pushing God aside as bills, unmet expectations, and obligations mount. We squeeze God in when time allows or when we're unable to claw our way out of the valley we are trudging through.

I want to ask you a question: Amid all the busyness, where does God fit?

This may not be a typical question asked when trying to remove the clutter and clear our vision, but I believe it is the right place to start. I am also not ramming him into this narrative. Our behaviors, the way we react to circumstances, and how we order our daily life could imply that God belongs on the back burner on low heat. We want to keep the water hot, while playing hopscotch with the relationship or effort.

Like Saul, Israel's first king, who tried to kill David, we start with good intentions but soon begin building our own tiny kingdoms atop quicksand. We find ourselves needing to prove our value and feeling disconnected from God, even while everything is going up in flames all around us—we're looking to others or things for fulfillment, justifying our actions or decisions, and then finding someone to blame when everything ends poorly.

Our calendars keep us preoccupied, providing built-in excuses to disengage from what really needs to be addressed. Children, trauma, work, the longing for more—all of it sets the groundwork for priorities to become idols. All the distractions and necessary commitments kept me mired in failure and regret, stuck in familiar but unbeneficial habits. In part, our perception of the world around us and how we move through it can be the root of the problem.

How we determine what is important to us influences how we show up and see the world. This can also impact how we believe God responds to our plans. Reread that: *How we believe God responds to our plans directly impacts how we see him.* And when *our* priorities become the only priority, we think our priorities are the same as God's priorities. So, I ask you again, where does God fit?

This is not about wedging him into your life based on convenience, but expanding your vision of him and understanding the benefits of engaging God in the mess and clutter, the mundane and frantic schedules. Consider Matthew 11:30. If you've never read this verse, God states, "My yoke is easy, and my burden is light." The yoke referred to in this verse is a piece of farming equipment attaching two animals, usually oxen, together, allowing them to bear the load together.

What Jesus offers us here is an invitation to allow him to guide our steps. Depending on the season, this could mean leading you toward pockets of more rest or mental relief, walking with you through trauma, or helping you clear those hurdles you keep stumbling over. The point: you are no longer carrying the weight of life's load, chasing unnecessary deadlines, or living an exhausted life with no end in sight. There is a helper, Jesus, who is an ever-present help, ready to take on our burdens.

Life is full of complexities, and along the way, we pick up things we were never meant to carry. The thought of handing our clutter over to God may provoke an eye roll, but stay with me here. I understand you are overwhelmed. I could have jumped right to the quick solutions, but foundation matters. If the ground you stand on is shaky, cracks will appear. The list of work and life issues and responsibilities is not going anywhere.

Considering God on the front end engages the mind and spirit in a different way when trying to tackle bills, trauma, worry, and hopelessness. Just pushing through is not the answer; nor is finding new ways to create lists, and you know it. Matthew 11:28–30 invites us to involve God proactively and hand things over.

BREAKING THE LOOP

Now that we have set our feet on a solid foundation, let's work toward grounding ourselves in peace even amid the chaos of our schedules. We should certainly plan, prepare, and prioritize. But if the solution is to pick up everything we or someone else deems important, when is there space to breathe, grow, or simply say "no more"?

It's time to break the loops of failure and regret that trap us and keep us from facing forward. We do this by asking three questions. These are questions we should ask when creating new practices and also when considering disrupting current ones. Ask the following:

1. Is this important?
2. Why is it important?
3. Who decided it was necessary?

Surprise, surprise, we are back to you deciding the answers. Not me, your mentor, or your community leaders. You are capable of this, one day, one task, and one failure at a time. Let's go through a quick exercise together, right now.

Think about a critical priority in your life. Not something someone else deems a priority but an item you have decided is important. Think through *why* it is crucial. There is no wrong answer. Now, who decided this was necessary? Now riddle me this, when was the last time you asked God if the item, idea, or rhythm (no matter how popular) you have introduced into your life is beneficial?

I am not judging your response. These questions aren't meant to cause shame but to place your feet back in the position of power. Remember, I started the book by telling you about when I stood in the rain talking to myself and the failures leading to most of these springboard questions. There is a benefit to being honest with yourself. You can shift your perspective and, where needed, move in a different direction.

I admit I tend to be reactive, especially when something appears useful or will lessen my emotional or mental load. For example, when faced with over-whelming stress, I may instinctively seek quick fixes or distractions to remove the discomfort, rather than facing the issue head-on. Pausing and answering the three questions mentioned, especially number three, is critical when deciding what makes each day's list. Seem too simple? It's not. Choosing is not always easy because there are many variables to consider. But deciding what is important helps us understand what holds the most value and why. In turn, it also helps us lead and show up better and move with confidence and live a life with fewer regrets.

As you go through the three questions, you might struggle to answer one or all of the above. I get it. But keep returning to these questions because the "why" is extremely important. They will also help you trim the fat off your current and future schedule. These questions are designed to interrupt the familiar and cause you to pause before adding another "solution" to your life. Not every solution will work for you.

Popular approaches to enhancing your life may do the opposite for you. Just like we should not change the core of who we are to fit the needs of others, we also should not allow others to manage the flow of our life. The goal is to move away from reacting and being overwhelmed to a place of clarity and control.

PRIORITY VERSUS OBLIGATION

In the midst of the chaotic juggle that was my life— parenting, work, personal commitments—I found myself wrestling with a fundamental question that seemed to exacerbate the struggle: Is there a difference between a priority and an obligation? The prevailing narrative insisted that everything is a priority, a belief that only intensified the difficulty of choosing which responsibilities to uphold and which to let slip away.

Parenting, in particular, became a battleground where last-minute work trips collided with doctor's appointments and recitals. And I faced disapproving glances of other parents when I arrived late to pick up my kids after practices. The pressure to conform to others' expectations added a layer of shame to the already complex mix. This internal conflict prompted a deeper exploration of the distinction between obligations and priorities. An obligation, I realized, tends to override personal wants and desires. While an obligation is always a priority, the reverse isn't necessarily true—a priority is not always an obligation. This realization was a game changer, placing the power of decision-making firmly back into my hands.

Sometimes we let our emotions dictate our decisions, but understanding the dynamics of obligations versus priorities empowers us to navigate the sea of responsibilities with a strategic mindset. It allows us to make intentional choices in business planning, emotional investments, and personal relationships— all without succumbing to shame.

We're all obligated to meet certain responsibilities, and determining whether something is an obligation or a priority enables us to decide with confidence what stays and what can be delegated elsewhere. We can begin doing things proactively because we aren't weighed down by the unnecessary. We put shame in its place because we have decided what is important, instead of letting someone else decide. When we label something as an obligation, it changes the conversation because we've drawn a line, declaring its importance.

Remember, crucial in this process is the recognition that an obligation is always a priority, but a priority doesn't always equate to an obligation. Finding a distinction between these two categories, as I did, is possible, especially when you engage God in what is being classified as essential. Be sure not to rush through the exercise of deeming what is important, even when what is important appears obvious.

I began changing my mindset back when I was a single mother, on the brink of financial ruin after my divorce. So no, it wasn't easy. I had to work on reminding myself to slow down and engage God. This did not happen until I personally understood the benefit of discerning between obligations and priorities. This was truly a process of self-discovery during a time that t felt very chaotic, but ultimately allowed me to reclaim power and control over my life.

Yes, you are bogged down, which is why instead of inundating you with a bunch of new ideas and practices to help you manage the chaos, I am giving you a few questions to help clear the decks where possible. We know there are no bulletproof solutions, but finding the right ones for you will require a level of resolve. In some cases, significant change over time.

There are a lot of variables to consider. And I am willing to acknowledge the difficulty and give you the permission slip to pause or change your mind, but there are no excuses being handed out. When you rush, you miss things. You end up sprinting without a plan or clear vision. But you know by now, there is no outrunning what is not faced head-on, even when everything is falling apart.

How we believe God is responding to our plans directly impacts how we see him. Engaging God proactively in our plans transforms our perception of him from a distant authority figure to a relational presence. Knowing what to prioritize and what to leave behind is the first step in a clutter-free life. A clear mind matters more than the forced balancing act of needs and desires, so trim the unnecessary baggage from your life by discerning the difference between an obligation and a priority. There's no reward for juggling "everything."

NINE

MIRRORS AND BREADCRUMBS

KNOWING THE REAL YOU

You'd think that after thousands of miles of globe-trotting, my body would have adjusted to last-minute red-eye flights from LAX to Columbus, Ohio. Not the case. After every red-eye, I would find myself dragging my limbs toward home, as if it were my first time traveling coast-to-coast.

This particular day, as I climbed the tiled steps to my doorway, my nerves bounced from pure exhaustion and what felt like a semitruck sitting on my chest. By the time my feet hit the entryway, gravel had once again nestled in the dips of my eyelids. Every fiber of my body was weighed down with regret. Regret from a week of meetings, a rigorous flight schedule, days without seeing my kids, heading into another weekend without plans, and facing the unanswered emails and the list of people my team would soon be firing from their jobs weighed heavily on me.

After I hauled myself up those stairs, I dropped my carry-on bag by my bed and made a beeline for the bathroom. It was there, in front of the mirror, that I caught sight of my reflection. Though life can be a blur, occasionally a seemingly mundane event will capture us, pulling us toward a lesson without our permission. Moments like these bring everything to a standstill and also into focus and force us to confront the direction we are headed, questioning whether we are satisfied with who we are becoming.

The reflection staring back at me seemed foreign, almost distant. I felt separated from myself, as though I were seeing someone else. The person in that mirror conveyed no joy or hope. With pained silence, I moved closer to the mirror, leaning in so tightly my breath fogged up the glass. I noticed my dazed pupils and the gray hairs that had begun weaving poetically among the brown, blond, and cinnamon-colored curls adorning my head. But it was what lay beneath that crown of curls that caused my stomach to drop to the soles of my feet.

I was looking at parts myself stuck in what felt like the belly of hell, a place only Jesus can reach, where we hide the parts of ourselves that cause us so much distress. In this place, tears of pain or regret fill our eyes, while anger simmers, leaving us to wrestle with whether to turn away from God, hold fast, or give up altogether.

Staring back at me was the face of a battle-worn person who had witnessed and experienced the unthinkable for almost ten years. She had survived, yes, but was still toying with giving it up—because surviving does not equate to victory. Sometimes it means navigating through even more volatility and struggle, digging deeper trenches.

The struggle to merely survive, to endure life without the quick, glossy finish, is not a popular Christian topic. What happens when we get to the other side of a situation and have to learn how to breathe with invisible weights still on our chests? There is no such thing as one-size-fits-all answers. Jesus never promised immediate healing, yet for some reason, we often expect it. Perhaps this is why it becomes so challenging to continue reaching and believing, even when we are leaning on Jesus.

In the mirror, I saw someone who had been abandoned and trapped in the cycle of compromise, weariness, and regret. I was lost, having handed myself over to distractions that kept me numb and stagnant. I needed Jesus to leave the ninety-nine and come back for me—not because of any overt sin or wickedness but because I had lost my way. Along the way, I'd crumbled. I released God's hand and replaced his love and ever-present help with busyness, the pressure to succeed, frustrations, and the roller coaster ride of competition.

But now, in that moment of clarity, I was seeing beneath the mask. And I saw a person who had been dragged through the mud, put on display, and propped up by the winds of pride. She had survived on the fumes of "I have no other choice."

Finally, I lost my grip. Thoughts raced and bounced through my mind. "I have no control over my life. No one has even consulted me about these lines making their presence known on my face. Who have I become? How did I get here?"

It is terrifying to see the real you, the person you've become after you've been through trauma, missteps, devastation, and sacrifice. Yet what unsettled me most was the stark realization that this time, I—not someone else—had left myself behind. I had followed the ups and downs of applause in an unfulfilling and endless loop, but the real me wasn't there.

Tears surfaced as I wrestled waves of discontentment, my unacknowledged rage causing sweat to bead on my neck as I reflected on all the times I should have made different, better choices. "How did I get here?" My thoughts raced through the memories of each time I had been mishandled, used, and cast aside.

But then the tears retreated behind the fears. Our questions need safe places to land, rest, die, or bloom into something wonderful. And I knew my mind wasn't a safe place for my unanswered questions right then. So, mechanically, I walked toward the shower, addressing none of the questions racing through my head. Later, as I climbed into bed, the blankets encasing me in an airy hug, my thoughts still raced, asking once again: "How did I get here?"

STRANGER DANGER

It does not matter what the illusions say or how distracted you are. In the silence, as you sift through the clutter, with the only omnipresent God, the real you emerges. Whoever you are in these moments *is* an integral part of the authentic you. It's critical to acknowledge the rawness we feel within our imperfection is because many solutions are found when striving for achievement takes a back seat.

We all hide behind a version of something, wearing masks to navigate meetings, crisis, or the routines of daily life. Pretending is not just a game for children. But I'm not here to criticize. We all have reasons why we can't show up as our whole self in certain environments. The danger arises when we become entangled in the illusions, feeling safer there than in our reality. At some point the realization hits us: pretending can only last for so long.

What does it look like when the lamp guiding your steps is no longer God's voice and the echoes of promises whispered into the darkness, but rather the words and applause of others? How does it feel when life holds you hostage, forcing you into submission with eerie silence, ever-changing status quos, and overwhelming loneliness? It may resemble a stranger staring back at you in the bathroom mirror.

In many situations, pretending seems like the best or only option, especially when we are struggling. Morphing into versions of who others want us to be, running away from who we are becoming, and refusing to make eye contact with our choices is a game of chance with uncertain consequences. How long can we pretend before we lose ourselves?

If your life is chaotic, the goal here is to help you regain control. Part of this process involves deciding not to sprint toward the distractions, to stop pretending everything is fine, and to acknowledge that everything is not okay. There are no quick fixes to returning back to the core of who you are, no magic Bible verses that will take away all your problems in twenty-four hours.

The willingness to acknowledge who we are, alongside God, allows us to confront the shame of previous decisions, the defeat we attempt to evade, or the burdens of the current season. This approach, this level of honesty, is not only about facing forward but also about ensuring we remain anchored and do not lose the precious parts of ourselves as we strive toward better. And better with God is whole.

REALITY CHECK

The pretend you is never better. No matter what you've been told or how much you want to believe "fake it till you make it" provides a solid return, it rarely does, and the risk is not worth the potential reward. Every time you hide parts of who you are, delay healing, or compromise what you value, it comes at a cost. And sometimes this cost affects your perception of God.

Don't reject who you are for the pretender. That real you, not an illusion, is the one who should taste victory. All those years ago, I was in the midst of a major detour. I had broken off pieces of myself and hidden them away in an attempt to protect what had not been fully shattered. I became a hostage to my circumstances and the environments I moved within. I did what I felt necessary to protect my heart and mind.

These behaviors kept me not only from healing but also from drawing closer to God in my confusion and despair. I felt uneasy parenting two children and leading teams of people older than me, and I couldn't figure out how to manage the anger bubbling beneath the surface. "You gave me success, Lord, but there has been so much pain. So much loss. So much misunderstanding," I would think. Yes, the prayers of the righteous prevail, but they aren't always coated in praise, hope, or sweet poetry. Often they can be laced with despair and longing.

Pretending to be someone we're not, and losing

ourselves in the process, is sometimes the result of handing over pieces of ourselves to others or allowing others' perceptions to become our own. In previous chapters, we discussed compromise and what happens when we follow people to ledges, leaving us feeling stuck or asking, "How did I get here?" Now we need to delve deeper. To feel routinely emboldened in your life, knowing when to take the reins back is essential. Pay attention to when you are surrendering critical parts of yourself and neglecting to engage with God.

When we find ourselves in places of concession, we must pause to ask who or what influences us and the decisions we are about to make. One reason I no longer recognized myself in the mirror was because my reflection did not encompass all of me. Parts of me had morphed into what I had allowed to influence my mind and decisions. On my face were the imprints of the people I had allowed to alter my perception of myself.

For many reasons, I had relinquished control of who I was becoming, without concern for the destination, simply because it seemed easier than taking the reins myself. While some compromises were motivated by financial gain, others offered temporary rest from the exhaustion. I was so tired. Have you ever felt so drained that facing and accepting your reality for what it truly is didn't seem worthwhile? Doing what was expected became easier than critically thinking or pushing back. It was easier than facing the solitude day and night. Easier than having to explain myself. Easier than being understood and known. But easy also has a cost. Easy was moving me further away from my relationship with God.

Opting for surface-level acceptance may preserve our popularity, but beneath the facade, roots of inner turmoil will still grow. Each time we settle for ease over authenticity, subtle internal shifts occur, even if we can't immediately pinpoint them. When we begin altering ourselves for immediate gains, as I've observed not only in myself but also in leaders and professional athletes I've counseled over the years, we blend the misguided thoughts and beliefs of others with our own experiences and understanding.

The perspectives of others—our family and neighbors, business partners, friends, and "experts"—naturally intertwine with our thoughts. Like small pieces of lint sticking to a wool coat, these imprints may go unnoticed, seamlessly blending in with the original fabric.

However, when we do notice this fusion of external perspectives with our own, the ensuing tug-of-war between what others believe about us and what we know to be true becomes mentally exhausting. In certain environments, navigating all this becomes a necessary evil. Over time, fatigue sets in, and we find ourselves lost in the lie that "perception is reality." It is a slippery slope that keeps us from ever really standing upright.

The key to overcoming this challenge lies in owning your power to choose. You ultimately have the authority to influence what you see, who you become, how you change, your relationship with God, and the pace of your healing. To reclaim the power you have relinquished and move forward without the mental weights of perception may require openly communicating limitations, standing firm against popular narratives, and confidently asserting yourself, regardless of others' advice or how they may perceive you.

You can acknowledge your imperfections. Create the space needed to navigate the chaos of your life effectively. You are empowered to hit pause until you reconnect with the person reflecting back. I want you to walk in power and confidence, no longer dependent on the words of others, positive or negative. How do we achieve this? By deciding who has influence and discerning when to embrace or disregard someone's advice.

This is your life. Be vigilant in whose voices hold sway over your decisions and influence your path. By thoughtfully selecting who influences you and understanding their motivations, you maintain control over your power and confidence. It's about being intentional with whose opinions or advice you value and why. This deliberate approach will soon become natural, preserving your core values and providing the insights needed to make wiser decisions. Ultimately, it forces you to pause, listen, and understand both your own intentions and those of the individuals around you.

BREADCRUMBS OF PEACE

To delve deeper into this topic, consider the gap between the version of yourself perceived by others, who you aspire to be, and the person known by God. Let's start by focusing on your relationship with God, turning toward him not just once but repeatedly—with each new revelation, change of the year, or significant moment in your life. Real and lasting change rarely occurs until we draw closer to God.

Although it may appear simplistic or superficial at first glance, we understand it is far from that. The canopy of noise surrounding us exerts its influence, whether or not we realize it. Focusing on God diminishes the power and influence of that noise.

As I stood in front of the mirror, my stomach churning as I recognized the distance between who I really was and the person others were influencing me to become, I yearned for the assurance of God's presence. I imagined him, full of his goodness and glory, leaning against the wall beside me, beckoning me closer to him. I pictured him there, inviting me to remember that he is always with me in the storm, gently steering me away from regret. He pointed me toward breadcrumbs that would lead me to the answers I sought—subtle yet profound nudges toward his comforting presence and peace. These breadcrumbs embodied his whispers of reassurance, the glimmers of hope, and the gentle tugs at my heart, pointing me toward a deeper connection—a closeness found only in relationship—and a true understanding of my purpose.

We need real hope, not fluff. We need truth, not fleeting trends. Yet as we grapple with the grief of our dissatisfaction, we may struggle to reclaim hope.

Admitting this doesn't signify failure or weakness—it simply acknowledges our humanity.

I turned away from the mirror that day, just as we all do when we attempt to evade our problems. I did not pause to pray or talk with God. Not because I did not love him but because my fractured state made the practice feel foreign. Seeking relief from God did not feel like an option or a solution.

How often do we bury our heads in the shame? We avoid the path to sustainable freedom because we feel we have failed, that we must start again, or that we have zero clue what we are doing. How often do we turn away—not because of sin but out of humiliation and disappointment? We forget what safety feels like, so we chase the closest ghost found within our memory. We turn away from God and wrongly believe there is a fractured bridge between us and our Redeemer. And by continuing to turn away, we open ourselves up to struggles we can't anticipate, new worries, and fresh disdain for the present.

In my hurt, my mind convinced me that an ocean divide separated me from my Savior. I understood that feeling of relational distance all too well, having experienced it in my first marriage. Backs turned, oceans apart, with no words to bridge the chasm. It takes courage to move forward after facing rejection, experiencing failed ventures, or simply being stuck for too long. But God is not like people. And even amid my moments of distraction and distance, he never once turned his back on me. His faithfulness endured, drawing me back to him.

We always have a choice. We can keep doing what we've always done, or we can turn and take different steps. There is power in your pivot. So if you've been wandering or keeping God on the back burner, turn toward him. We are always invited to lean on God and run toward his embrace. And even when we don't readily respond to his whispers or acknowledge the beckoning in our spirit, he never turns away. He is always there for us.

God and his presence serve as the breadcrumbs guiding us back to peace and clarity, anchoring us as we work to keep our eyes forward while the chaos swirls. We will not find peace, worth, or understanding in the fleeting tasks in temporary relationships. Every moment of every day, God walks with us, always ready to draw near (Psalm 145:18). His presence reminds us of our significance, even as the mess and failures accumulate. His consistency beckons us toward real freedom when we are lost in the storms of life.

TREASURING THE REAL YOU

Years after facing my battle-worn reflection, I no longer carry the weight of the lies that once burdened my mind—those implanted by myself and others. I now walk carrying the ripple of a profound realization: God treasures the genuine me, not the facade others desire.

Jesus wants the unvarnished you, with all the imperfections, redos, and stutter steps. Even in your pretending, he sees, acknowledges, and loves you—the authentic you.

What aspects of yourself are you hiding, and why? Through each up and down in life, both successes and failures may necessitate shifts in your mindset and potentially in your relationships, including relationships with those individuals you have allowed to influence your decisions.

I can keep prompting you to face forward and grab on to hope, but if you struggle to confront the real you—the person cherished by God—you will continue to drift, out of sync, relinquishing control to others, perhaps the wrong people. So ask yourself, Do I want to be in control of my life? If the answer is no, remember this is a judgment-free zone, yet it's critical to pause and reassess. I've had my own moments when I did not want to be in the driver's seat of my life. I felt as though I couldn't get anything right, everything was heavy, and I couldn't calculate the consequences of even the smallest decisions. But you can't remain frozen in place. This is what happens when we relinquish control. We remain stuck in loops.

If your answer is a resounding yes, continue examining the disconnect between who you are, the person God sees, and how others perceive you. Learn to treasure the real you, and periodically revisit the questions outlined in this chapter. Answering those questions can anchor you to the truth about who you are and empower you in a way that feels authentic and manageable.

TEN

RECLAIMING YOUR VOICE

EMPOWERMENT

I am going to die. This time I am sure of it. All I can do now is prolong the inevitable by fighting the waves, thrashing with all my might against their power as I feel something invisible pulling me under. How did I get here? I'm in the middle of what feels like an endless ocean.

Surely, I will not make it to safety this time.

My arms are so tired, heavy from swimming and from what I had been carrying.

I feel the fear crawling along the chill bumps on my skin as I fight against being submerged. There is no sound, only dark waves with bursts of white.

I don't know how to tread water, and soon I will go under. I know the fear will pull me even deeper. Logic says I will lose this fight. There is no reason to cry out. Soon everyone will know I have drowned.

Glancing to the left and right, I see "1,000 feet" stamped on the side of a wall. Then I realize I am not in the ocean. I am in a pool. A surge of victory fills me as I realize I can swim to safety. I can save myself by swimming to the ledge.

1,000 feet to safety.

1,000 feet to the ledge.

1,000 feet until I can breathe freely again.

So I swim, pounding the waves with the limbs God gave me. But each stroke only creates more distance between me and freedom. My arms ache with exhaustion, and the ledge seems even farther away now. In an instant, I find myself under the dark waves, still fighting. I see bursts of light from the surface; that must be Jesus, I think as I glance to the left and the right.

Then with one last desperate thought and a final burst of energy, I realize I will not make it.

It is too late. I am drowning, and no one is here to save me.

I awake from this nightmare, gasping for air.

This recurring dream has haunted me since my midtwenties, a time when I really began to take in other people's thoughts and opinions. Over time, I lost touch with my own identity as I deflated under the weight of conforming to certain narratives. The weight of expectations, coupled with the use of intimidation tactics, icy silence from leaders to assert dominance, and passive-aggressive disrespect was a recipe for disaster.

In this atmosphere, I lost my courage, a vital trait for navigating life's storms and learning quickly from the challenges knocking us off-balance. The rattling happening internally provided a pathway for others' beliefs about me to shape my self-perception, affecting not only my sense of self-worth but also my confidence in my intellect, creativity, leadership, and parenting.

Suddenly being accepted meant bending toward the whims of approval, once again prioritizing others' opinions over my own voice. I was drowning in a sea of approval-seeking behavior.

I invite you to join me as we create new stepping stones toward feeling empowered, breaking free from the silencing forces and embracing the courage to speak up unapologetically, so those things we struggle to say in the daylight don't find their way into our dreams.

BREATHE FREELY

In many environments, we often find ourselves stifled, our voices drowned out by louder ones or bullied into silence. We hang our heads low and clench our fists in frustration, grappling with the lack of space for our thoughts, words, and perspectives.

There are many reasons others confine us to the boxes they've constructed, including a desire to control, a lack of awareness, a fear of competition, or a thirst for power. It's easy to see the harm in their actions, yet sometimes we succumb to their ways.

When we grant others permission, they impose their limitations on us, stripping away our ability to advocate for ourselves and leaving us feeling unheard or misunderstood. In work dynamics, this permission is not always straightforward; it can sneak in through the company culture, power dynamics, or unspoken expectations. Soon we have lost our voice and find it challenging to feel understood or acknowledged. Online, anonymous voices stand ready to dictate our emotions, prescribe our beliefs, and warn of the obstacles we'll face if we dare to deviate from the masses.

As we fold inward, the spaces to pressure-test these imposed perspectives shrink. This makes it increasingly difficult to challenge negative thoughts or practice assertiveness. Consequently, people, situations, and interactions stay in perpetual draft mode, awaiting constant edits, changes, adjustments, or corrections to fit the ever-shifting status quo.

Understanding why you struggle to speak up and how to move forward in conflict can be hard. But today, right now, I urge you to reclaim what is rightfully yours—what God declares as yours. You are meant to breathe freely above the waves, not to suffocate under a shroud of silence. You have the right to think out loud, process thoughts, and own your mistakes without the weight of others' opinions. Seize your voice, your power, and your strength. Choose to elbow your way back into the driver's seat of your life.

You don't have to surrender portions of your power to avoid conflict or maintain a false peace. You don't need to compromise your voice to appease others. You don't have to carry the dead weight of others' thoughts on your back. When we yield to pressure or allow others to silence us, we gradually forget the liberating feeling of speaking with unbridled freedom. It's time to declare, "Enough!" Awaken from the intoxicating fog that others have cast upon you. Unravel the lies that entangle you in broad daylight and disturb your peace at night. You've surrendered and sacrificed too much already.

Let's face it—the habit of silence breeds misery, a departure from the divine intent for your life. Take a moment now to reflect on three areas where you've compromised, whether in your character, dreams, purpose, or joy. It's time to reclaim those lost aspects of yourself. As we progress through this chapter, let's delve into three crucial points to empower you in reclaiming your voice:

1. **Confront your insecurities:** Gain a profound understanding of your insecurities so that they no longer hold dominion over you.
2. **Embrace failure:** Acknowledge openly the necessity of failing, as it is through these failures that true strength and authenticity emerge.
3. **Cultivate resilience:** Embrace resilience as a guiding force, allowing setbacks to shape you into a stronger, more empowered version of yourself.

CONFRONT YOUR INSECURITIES

I worked alongside a man named Tom for many years. This experience sheds light on the impact insecurities can have both personally and professionally. Tom, a smart and capable business partner, faced internal struggles that influenced his communication and decision-making.

His choices became less about achieving the best outcomes and more about avoiding any perceived flaws that he believed overshadowed his capabilities—flaws that were largely invisible to others. Consequently, Tom's business relationships suffered and his leadership abilities were questioned. His decisions were clouded by a biased perspective that he crafted, leading to a lack of consideration for his peers and the teams he led.

Conversations with Tom resembled amateur tennis matches, with challenges tossed back and forth but no real progress made. His personal insecurities had taken the driver's seat.

Reclaiming your voice, as illustrated by Tom's experience, involves confronting your insecurities. It's about resisting the takeover of self-doubt and negative self-talk. Allowing these internal struggles, including perceived shortcomings or unspoken anxieties, to dictate your decisions can lead to overcompensation. To bring this closer to home, imagine constantly doubting your abilities despite receiving praise or recognition and overworking yourself or sacrificing your well-being in the process. The more you attempt to compensate for your perceived shortcomings, the further you drift from yourself.

Breaking free from old chains, especially those rooted in insecurities, is a challenge, one that isn't resolved overnight. In countless coaching conversations, I've realized that many of us experience the struggle of fighting against the whisper of doubt.

Let me share a personal story about confronting an insecurity.

Back when I was in elementary school, I had a heavy lisp. The ridicule I faced from teachers led me to carry this insecurity into adulthood, affecting how I presented myself in business meetings. It became a habit to ask short questions or remain silent, avoiding anything that amplified the echoes of past prejudices. Yet God intervened, sending someone who pushed me beyond what I considered a limitation. This person helped me recognize how my insecurity was distorting my vision, urging me to wipe clean the foggy lens through which I saw myself. By acknowledging and addressing our insecurities, we pave the way to a more authentic and empowered self. I reclaimed my power, over time shook off a deep-seated insecurity, and removed the sticky weights others had placed on me.

The lesson here is not to downplay the legitimacy of our insecurities but to face them. They have a profound impact on our self-perception, relationships, and even our understanding of God's love for us. Rather than ignoring them, we must confront them, understanding the "what" and "why" beneath the surface. This involves doing the work, which may take the form of going to therapy, leaning on your community, adjusting your behavior, or setting boundaries. In acknowledging and addressing our insecurities, we pave the way to a more authentic and empowered expression of our voices.

EMBRACE FAILURE

No matter the season—be it the mundane day-to-day or the exhilarating climb to the peaks we seek—failure walks alongside us, a constant companion. It's something we all walk with, intimately entwined with the fabric of our existence. Yet many of us shy away from exposing our gaps, attempting to cloak our incompleteness from the world. This facade, this attempt to hide our failings, can wear down even the strongest of us, leaving us weary and defensive.

But if you truly desire to reclaim your voice, overcome this fear, and embrace failure, it is critical to adopt what I call the bounce back mindset. Yes, you will fall flat, and some moments will sting more than others. Some failures will have consequences that feel like a tidal wave of regret. However, when you acknowledge your ability to bounce back, you discover the essence of failing forward. Both are about landing with the intention of rising again.

I used to avoid failure as if it were a land mine, fearing that a single misstep would obliterate everything I had worked for. This fear haunted my dreams, pushing me to fail in private and conceal even the smallest mistakes. But the pretense of having it all figured out, even in the company of safety, left me drowning. Ego, fear, and immaturity pulled me away from my center, closer to cliffs representing my deepest fears, gradually eroding my sense of stability and confidence.

CULTIVATE RESILIENCE

To fail freely, we must cultivate resilience, another enduring quality that acts as a rubber band, helping us to fight, overcome, and double down with whatever grit remains.

When you can fail openly, without the desperate drive to appear perfect, your internal power increases. You can show up authentically, unapologetically. You have courage to speak up without fear of ridicule, over time making it a little harder for the world to push you around.

Reclaiming your voice is about removing fear with action, not just thoughts. Picture yourself at a social gathering where the conversation turns into a topic you're passionate about or have an opinion that counters the group. We have all been there, whether at dinner parties, work events, or during a social outing. In the past, you might have stayed quiet, nodding as the discussion moved along, suppressing your own thoughts, afraid of saying the wrong thing.

But as you work toward reclaiming your voice and asserting your ideas and opinions, the fear that once may have kept you silent becomes a mere whisper. This fearlessness not only empowers you to express yourself but also facilitates deeper learning and growth.

This transformation is gradual, requiring time and a reevaluation of what truly matters to you. The unsteady waves of doubt no longer dictate your actions, and those imposing limitations on you are no longer welcome.

Wisdom calls for leaning into, not away from, the people attempting to silence you. Yes, throw your shoulders into the chaos, disrespect, and silent insecurities that seek to knock you off course. Recognize the inherent power within you, fortified by God's presence and the support of those closet to you. Your voice is a reflection of your character and endowed with unwavering strength. Stand resolute, facing forward, readying yourself for the bounce back. Do so with a clear mind and open arms. In this journey of reclaiming your voice and hope, you are empowered to speak your truth boldly. Embrace resilience as a guiding force, no matter how it shows up, and allow setbacks to shape you into a stronger, more empowered version of yourself.

ELEVEN

RESISTANCE

IDENTITY UNVEILED

"You do not have the pedigree to be here."

I had spent fifteen years overcoming obstacles, breaking barriers, and navigating challenging conflicts. Now inside a beautiful marble building in downtown Chicago, I found myself seated across from yet another person who felt qualified to question my worth and challenge my qualifications.

This man I had spoken to only once before, armed with all his degrees and corporate know-how, was evaluating my worth and value based on tests and what he deemed appropriate. And he had clearly decided there was nothing significant about me. According to him, my experiences, though unique, were not prestigious enough to have propelled me this far. My choice not to obtain a Harvard Executive MBA or attend the Cornell Executive Leadership program made zero sense to him. He drew many conclusions, swiftly.

What he didn't know was I, too, was drawing several conclusions about him. Considering his words, he was either attempting to prove an assumption or provoke me into a response before the coffee in our cups had a chance to cool. I knew what it felt like to be baited—and I was for sure being baited.

The bait on the hook can take the form of disapproval, hatred, a slight, or an insult. The bait can be a side-eye, rudeness cloaked in audacity, or lack of appreciation of the effort it takes to do something. This display of another person's emotions can pull us in, causing a volatile stirring within us. Our insecurities roar toward the surface. Unmanaged anger is switched into overdrive as we feel the need to defend ourselves. Previously unchecked thoughts and emotions, though untrue, now appear valid.

I wasn't going to take the bait. With the "how" and "why" of my career and personal life being analyzed, I was not going to do anything that would further this man's scrutiny or reinforce his assumptions. His insults were not going to move me. I was not going to fall into the trap of matching the energy being projected onto me. Though I had solved little in my life, I was learning the benefits of being in control amid the chaos, failure, and misunderstandings that come with living. Even as things were crumbling real-time.

Instead of reacting, I sat in silence, drinking my now cold coffee. As I did so, I felt a calm wash over me. It's not that I wasn't upset, shocked by his audacity, or bothered. I was now putting into practice what I had told many others as they sat in my office seeking advice. Under pressure, I was allowing the silence to do the work. While being judged, I was okay with being misunderstood. As my professional history was flipped on its head, I embraced all the failure that led me to this chair in downtown Chicago.

By the time he let those biting words out of his mouth, I had learned to appreciate the space between a period and the start of a new sentence. I understood with every fiber of my being that not everything warrants a response. Even when the words are false and meant to evoke a reaction.

We have all heard the saying "You are in charge of *how* you respond." I want to add another critical element to these words of wisdom: You also get to decide *when* you respond.

THE POT STIR

In the ebb and flow of our daily lives, peace can swiftly morph into chaos when the people and situations around us trigger a harsh reaction, a retort that feels justifiable in the moment. The motivations behind people's words and actions often remain elusive, leaving us grappling with the mystery of their choices, their reluctance to apologize, or their failure to seek understanding before verbalizing their conclusions.

This dynamic is not confined to the workplace; it permeates our interactions in coffee shops, during errands, at the gym, and everywhere people congregate. When someone perceives themselves as "more deserving" or superior, it creates a combustible mix that can lead to potential disaster.

Each day, we navigate encounters pushing us to the edge, compelling us to justify our decisions, explain our feelings in exhaustive detail, and elaborate on the nuances of our "no" or the reasons behind our hesitation to immediately say "yes." In these moments, my father's wise counsel echoes: "You do not have to do anything, and you do not owe anyone an immediate response."

Choosing not to match the energy of others isn't

passive-aggressive; it's a personal flex—a demonstration of willpower. Opting not to engage in a back-and-forth exchange between someone else's expressed feelings and your own emotions is an act of wisdom. Ecclesiastes 7:9 serves as a guiding principle: "Do not be quickly provoked in your spirit, for anger resides in the lap of fools." This isn't about apathy; it's about discerning what is truly worth your time and when the power of silence can be a strategic lever.

People will attempt to undercut and deter you. Stand firm; do not be detoured. Reject any thoughts that paint you as less than valuable based on others' opinions. Refuse to minimize the divine guidance you've received. Do not be swayed by fools. There are times when your uniqueness and innovation are not meant for everyone to understand or witness fully.

Often people have no idea what they're talking about—an opinion, after all, is just that, not a fact to be acted upon. Recognize when to cradle your uniqueness and innovation, holding them close without offense.

Remember, you aren't obligated to share every feeling or experience, react, or justify your actions. Approval from bystanders, naysayers, or those uninvested in your well-being is unnecessary. Draw a firm line here and consider this your permission slip: no more allowing others to rearrange your steps or fill your thoughts with shame. It's time to reclaim the power to anchor yourself, standing tall in the knowledge of who you are and resisting the forces that seek to diminish your worth.

UNSHACKLED

Great teachers, leaders, and mentors not only bring out the best in us but also illuminate the gaps in our understanding, providing us with sustainable tools to navigate and course-correct. While our foundational leaders, such as parents and mentors from our youth, play a crucial role, we also need the wisdom, boldness, and seasoned guidance of individuals who can amplify our strengths and identify areas in need of pruning for our growth.

Denise, my mentor, has profoundly impacted my life. During moments of complexity in which money, emotions, and influential players intertwined, she imparted invaluable lessons with simple but provocative statements. Her words became rallying cries within my spirit.

In one such instance, as I felt my credibility hanging in the balance, Denise's guidance cut through the noise. With a simple yet powerful statement—"Never allow yourself to be held hostage"—she addressed the unspoken fears swirling in my mind: *What if they don't listen? What if they don't work with me anymore? What if people don't like the decision?*

At the precipice of my uncertainty, Denise reminded me that I am, in fact, unshackled. She urged me not to flinch in difficult situations and granted me the permission to take control. While her words didn't offer an immediate solution, they granted me freedom. They provided the space to think amid the rush and decide whether I wanted to be a leader or a follower.

Leadership is about deciding how you want to show up and doing it consistently. It's entails demonstrating integrity when no one is looking and course-correcting even when nothing is on the line. Leading requires repeatedly affirming to yourself that you are not, nor have you ever been, a hostage to the thoughts, feelings, and plans of others. You have the power to hit the pause button and reflect.

We may face situations where someone is questioning our capabilities, parenting, relationships, or career advancements. Yet, the appropriate response isn't always about proving others wrong; sometimes it's about maintaining and preserving internal peace.

Denise played a pivotal role in loosening the binds of business pressures, self-imposed consequences, and personal agendas. Now I extend the same opportunity to you—to snatch the reins back. Lead differently, change your mind, go against the grain, or take the time needed to process your thoughts. Creating space for silence, allowing words to land, and stretching within the process all foster the growth of wisdom's roots. Not everyone will appreciate your answers or welcome your thoughts. There will be situations where you stumble into deep trenches. Nevertheless, remember this:

You are not hostage to a job.

You are not hostage to a relationship.

You are not hostage to abuse.

You are not hostage to anything that is not good for you.

You are not hostage to loneliness.

You are not hostage to the status quo.

Don't forget: God has never declared any of us beholden to the things that threaten to keep us beneath the waves of depression, anxiety, stagnation, or frustration. You are not hostage to your failures.

Take Denise's words, and collaborate with God to begin unlocking the chains that have bound you.

Keep in mind, this journey will not unfold overnight. Just as it took years for me to navigate the tumultuous sea of emotions, it will also take you time to pick yourself up, face forward, and keep reclaiming hope. And when you lose your footing amid the fiercest winds and raging storms, remember that God's hand is there to guide you back to peace and purpose. Keep looking for the breadcrumbs.

In the journey to reclaim your voice and stand tall in the face of challenges, the struggle to discern how and when to react can be overwhelming. When you find yourself off-balance, outnumbered, or outwitted, if you do nothing else, harness the power of silence and remember to lean on God.

You are not alone in this process. Embrace the unfolding of your strength and resilience. The chains may have been tightly wound, but with God by your side, you possess the strength to loosen them and eventually break free. This will not be immediate. This will be a process, and the result will be a testament to your unwavering power.

Moving forward, remember you aren't tethered to the past or constrained by the challenges that once seemed insurmountable. Reclaim your voice, embrace the power within, and let the echoes of your strength resound as you move confidently toward your future.

LEAN

In the storms of life, greatness, potential, and excellence can't be predicted. People will inevitably misjudge you, for their perceptions are confined to the limitations of their own narratives. Some may dismiss you because your story doesn't neatly fit their expectations—it might be either too much or not captivating enough. Regardless, people will always find ways to rationalize their judgments.

But here's the secret: let them underestimate you. Don't invest your precious time trying to prove them wrong. Resist the pressure to justify your presence, and never apologize for the decisions you've already discussed and agreed upon with God.

Lean on Jesus. Not merely by following his footsteps but also by trusting the invaluable lessons embedded in past failures. Often overlooked are the verses reminding us that he goes before us, clearing a path based on his perfect work, our unique gifts, and earnest prayers. You, my friend, are an indispensable thread in his grand tapestry.

Emotional readiness for life's unpredictable turns is rooted in a relationship with the One who is never caught by surprise. I'm not talking about scraping by for resolution in intense moments; I'm talking about the peace that comes from having an ongoing relationship with God, knowing that he fills the gaps. *Where we are weak, he is strong.* These words guide us through the unforeseen, offering comfort in the face of uncertainty. Leaning on God's infinite wisdom isn't a sign of weakness—it's a courageous assertion.

Power dynamics shift when we respond thoughtfully to situations meant to rattle us. Confidence grows with clarity, and wisdom blossoms when we are guided not by our emotions provoking us but by God.

You are under no obligation to participate in the mind games others play—whether in the workplace, in friendships, or in intimate relationships. You don't have to be drawn into chaos or pulled toward other people's cliffs of despair and hopelessness. I have a personal mantra I use when my emotions threaten to take over and clarity is elusive: "Pull up!"

Pull up! When emotions try to take the driver's seat.

Pull up! When the urge to react is overwhelming.

Pull up! When things seem to be spinning out of control.

If you don't have your own phrase, feel free to borrow mine. Eliminate the desire to explain, justify, or prove your self-worth. The cycle of constantly needing to explain and seek validation is mentally taxing. When hurt, we rush to our own defense, explaining our decisions and telling our version of events. But responding hastily, without creating space, often causes us to miss the root issue. If you want your words to have impact, resist the urge to explain them away.

EMBRACING THE POWER OF SILENCE

Silence holds a profound strength that often goes unnoticed in a world clamoring for constant noise. When we resist the urge to hastily explain the impact of others' words, we create space for the transformative power of silence to unfold. This silence offers a rare opportunity to see things clearly, liberating us from the influence of overpowering emotions.

Certainly, some may take issue with your choice not to respond immediately. The discomfort it stirs may be palpable, as was evident in the Chicago meeting where my lack of immediate responsiveness was not perceived as stoic, but indifference.

Yet your silence is not an invitation for disrespect or uninformed assumption; it is merely silence.

Consider this: What are your expectations of silence? Understanding your desired outcomes from moments of quietude transforms the seemingly mundane into a strategic advantage, elevating rest and improving execution. Silence is not about escaping; it's about introspection, allowing God's voice to resonate, regaining composure and hope amid personal chaos, and responding with intention.

There's another facet to this silence—you must be comfortable with not always being understood, heard, or agreed with. Embrace stillness as an opportunity to observe and assess, to listen for the voice of God, and to grow without the noise of external opinions. Sometimes all it takes is five minutes to think, to adjust, to find the courage to say you need more time. In its purest form, silence closes the gap between ideas, people, or desired outcomes, creating room for change and growth.

NAVIGATING THE AFTERMATH

"Thank you for your time."

I shook the man's hand, silently hoping I'd never

see him again, and headed toward the elevator. Entering the waiting car, I requested that the driver take the scenic route back to the hotel, craving the solace of my own thoughts.

In the solitude of the car, self-doubt crept in, fueled by the sting of audacious judgments. Questions lingered as we wound through Chicago's streets: Were my goals misplaced? Did this stranger truly know me better than I knew myself? In the silence, I sifted through the events of the day, focusing on the moments where I held form:

- choosing assertiveness over aggressiveness
- maintaining my character in the face of audacity
- taking ownership of my responses

As the car made one final turn, I wrapped myself in the warmth of my coat, an acknowledgment of both winter's chill and the weight of the day resting on my shoulders. Knowing ourselves better than anyone else is a crucial milestone where external opinions become secondary.

However, even armed with hard-earned knowledge and resilience, I still found myself crumbling in the privacy of the hotel room, tears flowing freely.

Life isn't a cinematic montage or a series of inspirational quotes rescuing us from turmoil. When judgment or shame confronts us, it can be challenging to dodge, even with Jesus by our side. The sting may linger, but even as we fall apart, it's essential to acknowledge the hurt. Then we must gather our strength and keep facing forward, standing resolute in our truth. In these moments of brokenness, audacity, or struggle, remember this:

You are not a hostage.

You do not have to respond.

Allow silence to do the work.

A CONCLUSION

THE POWER OF PAUSE

The clouds were rolling in, heavy with the promise of rain. "Maybe I can get a run in before the kids wake up," I thought. My entire family was on our annual summer vacation in Charleston, South Carolina. One house, with many rooms, every moment filled with laughter and love.

The mornings were a time when the adults could sneak off and sit on the deck, stare at the pool water while whispering about the plans for the day, drink coffee while it was still hot, and in my case, sprint across the soft sand along Kiawah Island. As I softly closed the front door to the house, I caught a glimpse of my baby brother's wife rubbing his hair with affection. "He looks so much like our father in the mornings," I thought, taking in a deep breath.

I could smell the storm but couldn't see it. I pulled my hair back tightly and at the last minute opted to wear the longer shirt I kept in the car.

I listened to the cadence of my feet hitting the pavement instead of music. As I turned the corner, the silence around me was peaceful—a familiar feeling in this season, my own life felt more grounded even as problems refused to fade. I turned another corner and ran down a long, paved pathway. The grass along the path was taller than an average man, so tall it reminded me of the bamboo I saw when traveling through China in my early twenties. I stopped and snapped a picture.

And then, as if right on cue, the rain began to pour, and I sat on the wet grass and snapped a photo of myself sitting in the rain, peacefully looking up toward heaven as the raindrops hit my shoulders. Instead of bouncing off me, they fell right into the warmth of my body. I continued my run, making my way to the beach, running at a quicker pace along the shoreline.

I was thinking about nothing and everything. Then the familiar voice of God repeated something softly, words he had said to me a year prior while I was on a road trip to Colorado: "The storm is not everywhere." I find God fascinating, especially how he can say something to us and the words arrest our spirit in the most tender way for the remainder of our lives. He provides answers in the present but also pulls us closer to him, deeper into the wonder and glory that is God.

I hauled to a stop, almost injuring my hip. The sand cushioned my shoes as the impact of old words snatched my present moment. When God had first uttered the phrase to me, I was driving in a literal storm. On my side of the highway, headed south, there was a downpour, but on the opposite side of the highway not a single drop of rain. The pavement appeared dry. Had there been no highway, I could have placed one foot in the storm and the other foot outside of it, straddling the line between chaos and calm. The moment captivated me; I pulled over and snapped a picture.

All the failures, restarts, and lessons learned had helped me snatch back the reins of my life. With God, I had reclaimed the right kind of hope without sacrificing what was precious—the values and beliefs that define the real me. Though storms still come, they appear slightly different, reminding me that while I might find myself in the midst of chaos, the storm is not all-encompassing. It may feel as though everything is falling apart, but the trenches are not as deep, and the cliffs not so alluring. The storms in life aren't the only thing happening around us. As we move forward with God, they will become either a springboard for growth or, if we choose, an unspoken footnote in our story.

I looked out at the ocean and noticed a clear sky. Not a single cloud obscured the vast expanse. The sunlight danced across the water's surface as if they were old friends embracing after being apart for too long. To my back, over the houses that littered this amazing island, the sky was adorned with countless clouds. They overlapped each other as if they were competing for space in a limited expanse.

"The storm is not everywhere," I noodled. Then I removed my wet, sandy running shoes and made my way toward the ocean. I walked until the mixture of salt, old and new life, and the storyteller of nature reached my knees. Then I stopped, allowing my feet to sink into the sand and the waves to twist around my legs and then rush away. There would be no more running today. No morning routine. No breaking of sweat before the sunlight wove its golden warmth into the day. Instead, I chose to pause in this moment, a profound contrast from those years ago when I stood mumbling in the rain and hope seemed distant. Wrapping my arms around my waist, I stood still, listened, and waited with a profound sense of peace in my heart.

STRENGTH IN STILLNESS

With every word shared on these pages, I trust you've discovered insights and stories that resonate with your own experiences, ultimately propelling you forward. Yet amid all the narratives, one theme stands out—embracing the power of pause.

Pausing is not merely about rest; it's the courageous act of introspection and surrender. It's about waiting patiently for God's response, even when the silence seems deafening. It is a decision to relinquish control and allow God to weave his purpose through our lives without resistance.

But this is no easy feat. It demands a different type of resilience, a steadfast resolve to let things unfold in their own time, resisting the urge to rush toward conclusions that tether us to relentless cycles of turmoil.

Deciding to move differently in your life isn't about insisting on perfect answers; it's about making room for different outcomes. It requires allowing God to flow through your life in unpredictable ways.

This is courageous work, attempting to stand still and face forward as turbulence shakes the ground beneath our feet, unearthing our deepest fears and insecurities.

There's no poetic fluff here, no quick fixes. Pausing and holding our ground demands unwavering resolve. Focus and grit are prerequisites for leaning on God when understanding slips away. Courage is needed when changing course, especially when the status quo no longer serves you. Let me encourage you with utmost clarity:

Facing forward requires risk and at times putting effort in multiple directions.

Progress is not a one-way street.

Reclaiming hope takes shape through various avenues and paths.

There are times when pausing may feel as though you are going backward, giving up ground. But periods of stagnation are not signs of defeat. Not hearing God's voice does not mean he is not teaching you something significant. You pause and wait, right where you are until the time is right. Until God gives the green light or you feel settled in your mind.

In the pause, there is grace—clarity, confidence, peace, and unyielding strength. It's within the stillness that we determine the perfect moment to pivot, find the answers we seek, bid farewell to our mess, and stare fear in the eye without blinking. In these moments, not rushed or flustered, we can finally embrace the strength hidden within our past failures.

You are more than qualified to change your mind, but pausing helps put regrettable actions behind you. Reject the illusion that progress is only attainable once we achieve success. Through hard-earned wisdom, personal struggle, and mentorship, I have learned time and time again that true growth is not confined to moments of triumph, but rather, it flourishes along the dusty parts of the journey—where only you and God can dwell. I also learned that pivoting isn't merely about changing direction or scattered thinking; it's a declaration—a way of saying, "This path no longer serves me."

By the time I was standing on that beach, under a sky painted with both clouds and sunlight, I had learned the hard way how detrimental it can be when we try to make superficial changes on the run or refuse to change at all. I discovered that God's voice will forever appear faint when we step away from his presence.

Pausing is not a sign of weakness; it's an act of grace toward yourself—an opportunity to reevaluate and realign our steps with God's guidance. Embrace the winding, and at times unpredictable parts, of your journey. Mistakes are inevitable, failure will happen, and certain strides may feel shaky once you start again. But I want you to gift yourself compassion and acknowledge that growth is inherently messy.

BRIDGES

Throughout these chapters, each story and lesson has served as a plank in the bridges we constructed over tumultuous waters, leading us to a profound realization—that when we face forward, no matter what is happening around us, God is the one looking back at us. His unwavering character remains steadfast amid every storm. With Jesus as our counterweight, we can navigate away from the chaos with our backs straight and heads held high, no matter how intense the storm may be.

We didn't construct these bridges solely with Bible verses, though we easily could have. Instead, stories of failure and reflection were used to help forge paths forward.

You might feel shaken after traversing these chapters, still grasping disappointment—that's natural. I made no big life-changing promises to you or offer bulletproof solutions beyond anchoring yourself to God, because only he can give us hope, a foundational self-identity, and clarity in the chaos of life.

So why end with bridges? Because we're all headed somewhere, being influenced. I want you to lead, grow, and learn, all while heading in the right direction. With grit, passion, and the lessons learned from failure, I believe you can achieve everything covered in this book and more.

By shattering the illusion of perfection, we build bridges toward God's "well done," reclaiming our voices and finding the courage to reorder our steps with eyes wide open. In the silence, we not only embrace the power of pausing but also realize we are not hostages in our lives; rather, we're shattering barriers with God and witnessing the ripples of courage.

So what's the *so what*? Now what?

New chapters bring new questions requiring a different type of faith leading toward deeper answers. As your perspective deepens, let the unchanging Word of God guide any shifts in behavior and thinking. Continually aim to be more like Jesus. Resist falling back into lifeless habits, regardless of their popularity. The goal is never to eliminate obstacles; that's impossible. Instead, never again allow fear or failure to manage or control you. Don't compromise your faith, wants, or needs simply to appease others.

As you close this book, trouble may be waiting. The storms may be blowing and the cliffs of what-ifs and regret may be calling, but there stands Jesus, refusing to leave you alone in your failures, compromises, or confusion. Even while working to regain control of your life, it is important to choose those who earn the right to walk alongside you. It is important to remember you are in the driver's seat.

I'm cheering you on through every trial and misstep. Not because I am watching from some great mountain of insight or perfection but because I know the power of failing well, bouncing back, and trying again and again.

By God's hand, bridges are created, and our anchors are meant not to weigh us down but to propel us forward. As you fix your gaze on God's unwavering promises and reclaim everything that is rightfully yours, remember this: the author of this book once stood unsteady, seeking hope in the rain. Yet, through faith and perseverance, she discovered peace and purpose in God's embrace. May this truth resonate with you as you turn your face forward, stepping boldly into the next chapters of your life.

ACKNOWLEDGMENTS

My heart overflows with gratitude for the remarkable individuals who have walked alongside me through this book's diverse chapters. Their influence has been immeasurable, and their support is invaluable.

To my agent, Trinity McFadden, your unwavering belief in this project has been its cornerstone. Your steadfast support and encouragement have breathed life into my dreams, and for that, I am eternally grateful. You remain a beacon of light in a sea of creative endeavors.

Ryan Pazdur, Alexis De Weese, Kim Tanner, and team, your wealth of knowledge has been a steadfast compass, navigating me through the complexities of this process. Without your expertise, this path would have appeared insurmountable. Your unwavering commitment to sharing insight and perspective speaks volumes to the depth of your character. You have each been a joy to work with.

Denise, Donna James, Luke Fedlam, Autumn Glover, Trista Troutman, Brittney Perkins, Kristy Etling and team, Cory Miller, Ivan Smith, and Jamie Schroder—you have been my strength and anchor throughout the years. In the tumultuous landscape of the corporate world, you stood as steadfast allies, guiding me through challenges with unwavering dedication. Your cheers echoed through the valleys of adversity, spurring me onward as I scaled towering peaks of obstacles. Your belief in me remained unshakable, and even as I embarked on a new journey, I will be forever indebted.

Mariela Rosario, Charaia Rush, Jasmine Holmes, Ainsley Britian, Tabitha Panariso, Elizabeth Zell, and Cynthia Maselli—your presence in my life is a constant wellspring of inspiration. Your support, each unique in its form, enriches my life profoundly. All of you fuel my determination and growth, and I am humbled by your impact. It is my honor to call you friends.

Ashley Abercombie, Jennifer Allwood, Cassandra Spear, KJ Ramsey, Kara Strout, Erin Moon, Vanessa Vera, Ariana Rivera, Pricelis Perreaux-Dominguez, Sajah Carter, Randi Fahle, Brittany Maher, and Jackie Aviles—I am grateful for your gracious support and encouragement. Thank you for being a listening ear and sharing your valuable perspectives throughout this process.

Steph, Nicole, Leslie, Liz, Doonie, Missy, and Gina—our bond transcends time and distance, woven together by the threads of shared experiences and unwavering support. Since 2002, we have weathered storms together, sharing our triumphs and tribulations. The women we have become is a testament to this friendship. Here's to the many more twists and turns that lie ahead. Thank you for being my lifelong friends and supporting me once again as I took another leap of faith.

Bobby and Jessie Lemley, your home in Charleston, South Carolina, provided the sanctuary to breathe life into these pages during the beginning stages. I will forever cherish the memories forged within your walls.

Zion and Londyn, my beloved children, you have witnessed your mother's journey through enduring rejection, facing stereotypes, and being minimized. Despite it all, you have seen your mother win but have not witnessed the countless tears shed, the frustration accompanying growth, the failures endured, and the moments when I gave up. My deepest desire is that this book provides a glimpse into the resilience required to persevere and rise again, even in the face of adversity. Keep your eyes forward, babies, and stay bold even when you have lost belief.

To my beloved husband, Joseph, my affection for you knows no bounds, and I am endlessly grateful for your presence in my life. Your love and unwavering support have enriched my life profoundly, and I am infinitely blessed to walk this life by your side.

Lastly, to my church family near and far, your influence has left an indelible mark. As I face forward, I carry a smile and hope. Thank you, from the depths of my soul, for being a part of what has been an incredible life thus far.